IMPLICATIONS FOR ACCOUNTANTS OF THE USES OF FINANCIAL STATEMENTS BY SECURITY ANALYSTS

This is a volume in the Arno Press collection

THE DEVELOPMENT OF CONTEMPORARY ACCOUNTING THOUGHT

See last pages of this volume for a complete list of titles.

IMPLICATIONS FOR ACCOUNTANTS OF THE USES OF FINANCIAL STATEMENTS BY SECURITY ANALYSTS

Charles T. Horngren

ARNO PRESS
A New York Times Company
New York • 1978

Editorial Supervision: LUCILLE MAIORCA

First publication 1978 by Arno Press Inc.

Reproduced from a copy in the University
of Chicago Library

THE DEVELOPMENT OF CONTEMPORARY ACCOUNTING THOUGHT
ISBN for complete set: 0-405-10891-5
See last lages of this volume for titles.

Manufactured in the United States of America

Library of Congress Cataloging in Publication Data

Horngren, Charles T., 1926-
Implications for accountants of the uses of financial statements by security analysts.

(The Development of contemporary accounting thought)
Originally presented as the author's thesis, University of Chicago, 1955.
Bibliography: p.
1. Financial statements. 2. Investment analysis.
I. Title. II. Series.
HF5681.B2H65 1978 657'.3 77-87301
ISBN 0-405-10940-7

THE UNIVERSITY OF CHICAGO

IMPLICATIONS FOR ACCOUNTANTS OF THE USES OF FINANCIAL STATEMENTS BY SECURITY ANALYSTS

A DISSERTATION SUBMITTED TO
THE FACULTY OF THE SCHOOL OF BUSINESS
IN CANDIDACY FOR THE DEGREE OF
DOCTOR OF PHILOSOPHY

BY
CHARLES T. HORNGREN

CHICAGO, ILLINOIS
MARCH, 1955

PREFACE

This dissertation attempts to present the implications for accountants of the uses of financial statements by security analysts. The study is based upon a survey of existing literature on investment analysis, plus interviews with security analysts in New York City and Chicago and scrutiny of their written analytical reports.

The security analysts have been extremely cooperative. They have taken ample time from their busy hours to discuss this study. They have been very generous in allowing this writer to inspect their confidential written reports, subject only to the promise that the sources of such reports be withheld.

Although the topics discussed in the interviews and in the analysts' written reports were many and varied, the specific passages from written reports and the quotations from personal interviews which are reproduced in the following pages were scrupulously chosen in order to reflect validly the views and the procedures of the analysts as a <u>group</u>.

TABLE OF CONTENTS

LIST OF TABLES

CHAPTER I

INTRODUCTION

A broad statement on the purposes for which accounts are prepared is included in the introduction to Accounting Research Bulletin No. 43:

> The test of the corporate system and of the special phase of it represented by corporate accounting ultimately lies in the results which are produced. These results must be judged from the standpoint of society as a whole--not merely from that of any one group of interested persons.[1]

Accounting provides useful information in three main fields: (a) management, (b) investment, and (c) government. All of them must be served as well as possible. The comprehensive question with respect to investors is "what information shall be published for their benefit?" This study attempts to indicate the answer to this question. Such an answer centers about the types and the amounts of information which may be *useful* to investors. Is all additional information to the good? Or is there a point at which all essential information has been furnished? Where is the point beyond which comes a period of rapidly diminishing returns from additional information provided?

If one seeks the answers to the above questions, he is

---

[1]Committee on Accounting Procedure, American Institute of Accountants, *Accounting Research Bulletin No. 43: Restatement and Revision of Accounting Research Bulletins* (New York: The American Institute of Accountants, 1953), p. 7.

led to resort to the opinions of security analysts and to the specific analytical techniques which they employ in dealing with financial statements. These questions cannot be answered in quantitative terms. Opinion testimony is needed as to the value to an investor of various items of accounting information. These opinions must be validated insofar as possible by examinations of the analytical procedures and analytical reports which are used by professional investors. In other words, specific written analyses of several companies must be scrutinized in order to ascertain what the financial analysts' approaches are to quantitative information.

Although this study concentrates upon financial statements and related quantitative information, it is recognized that this quantitative phase forms a part of a larger question as to the value of financial statements as a whole, as compared with other kinds of information such as the future of the industry and the ability of the management. It is easy to contend that each part of the information should be as accurate and reliable as it can be made. But there is also a question of setting up all the material information in a suitable proportion to the total amount of time which even careful investors can devote to the making of a single investment decision.

Purpose

This study attempts to appraise accounting from the viewpoint of the professional security analyst. In order to secure this viewpoint it was necessary to discover what the financial analysts' approaches are, especially with respect to their uses and interpretations of financial information. How do they deal with the uncertainties that emerge from sketchy data? What pet adjustments do they make to the data? What do they especially want but seldom get? What are the major shortcomings of accounting data with respect to its uses by investors? Do they, for the most part, avoid any painstaking analysis of accounting information? More specifically, this investigation has probed into questions such as the following:

1. What are the sources of the accounting data which you use?

2. What types of accounting data are of greatest use? That is, what types of data are almost invariably important in leading to your conclusions?

3. What types of accounting data are of little or no use?

4. What important deficiencies have you found with respect to supplementary statements and statistics?

5. What important deficiencies have you found with respect to accounting statements?

6. What accounting information do you want that ordinarily is not readily available, or that simply does not exist? For example, do you feel that replacement values of fixed assets and inventories held, and that commitments as to future expenditures are of great or little importance in your analysis?

7. Are there any favorite analytical tools (i.e., ratios, comparisons) that you frequently use in your analysis?

8. Are there some types of accounting information that you feel are especially important but that you rarely get?

9. What are the main improvements you consider to be most desirable in the accumulation or presentation of accounting data?

10. What techniques do you use to estimate detailed figures which are not available at the time of your analysis (i.e., revenue and cost breakdowns by product lines, sources and applications of funds)?

A survey of the existing literature on investment analysis, plus scrutiny of 123 written analytical reports and the collection of the opinions of 51 analysts in trust departments of banks, investment counseling firms, underwriting houses, insurance companies, investment trusts, brokerage houses, and investment research firms in New York City and Chicago have yielded some indications of the major uses of accounting information by security analysts. These findings have focused the spotlight on some accounting procedures and presentations which need appraisal.

Method and Scope

The heart of this study has been the scrutiny of the techniques used by security analysts in their analyses of published financial statements. It is believed that what security analysts actually do can be best discovered by studying the specific procedures they use in analyzing quantitative data, and by attempting to determine the reasoning from which they have developed those procedures.

The task of collecting the opinions of professional investment people with regard to the accounting information they receive is also an essential part of this investigation. It is contended that the most valid method of collecting these opinions is through personal interviews. It is maintained that the use of questionnaires and statistical tabulations based on scientific sampling would have missed the qualitative information that would be of the greatest value.

If one talks to a number of security analysts, reads the literature that they have written for publication, and examines their written analytical reports, a surprising similarity of opinion will be found with respect to the types of financial data that are important--those data which make a difference in a specific analysis of quantitative material. However, it is emphasized that this similarity of opinion does not mean that analysts are robots who do the same things with the same available data when studying a specific company.

Because of this similarity of opinion and approach, from the analysts' standpoint it seems that the accountant is not attempting to serve many investment masters. Rather, the composite analyst (the "all-American analyst") comes from a homogeneous group, all of whom are seeking information which will aid in their decision-making. Some are more vocal than others and some appear to be relatively more unhappy with the corporate information readily available--but essentially they want the same quantitative information and they try, within reasonable limits, to obtain this data via the most convenient avenues.

This discovery has been a fortunate one because the writer can present a summary of the analysts' standpoint almost without allowing for exceptions which might be taken by some analysts. In other words, it is strongly felt that the analysts' views presented in this study are generally applicable to nearly all analysts--that the analysts' views are clear-cut and definite, as a class or a group-position.

Presentation of this Study

This writer has attempted to summarize the analysts' point of view largely (a) by quoting what the analyst has written for publication, (b) by reproducing passages from his written analytical reports of specific companies, and (c) by quoting or paraphrasing the opinions collected in personal interviews. Sources of information have been cited specifically wherever possible, but in the cases of quoted excerpts from written analytical reports the sources have been withheld upon request because of the confidential opinions offered.

This study has been divided into two major parts. The first part (Chapters II-III) attempts to describe the analyst's position in terms of his wants and needs as a primary consumer of financial data. The second part (Chapters IV-VIII) tries to draw implications for accountants from the approaches of analysts to the most troublesome kinds of data. The types of data chosen for extended treatment were those which analysts generally felt to be the most important in the final analysis: inventories, non-recurring items, and fixed assets. It seems that an intensive study of the latter items would be more useful and meaningful than an extensive study of a large number of controversial items which are of lesser significance when viewed in perspective.

This writer feels that the most startling discovery in this investigation has been the 100 per cent stand of security analysts against the application of price-level adjustments to conventional accounting data. There is more to analysts' reasoning on this issue than appears at first glance. Analysts are not concerned with the changing purchasing power of the dollar because when examining income statements they think in terms of fund flows of current dollars. Analysts' views on this matter (Chapter VIII) deserve much more consideration than has been given to them by the proponents of adjusting conventional accounting reports for the changing price level.

It is not intended that this study be hypercritical of accounting practice and/or annual reporting practice. It seems to this writer that accountants are increasingly recognizing that useful standards of a meaningful kind are positively necessary if accountancy is to successfully perform its important task in our economic system. In recent years the American Institute of Accountants, the American Accounting Association, and the Securities and Exchange Commission have progressed with giant steps toward the development of accounting standards. The past twenty years have been marked by substantial improvement in the "independent" position of public accounting firms. But, as in every phase of business activity, there is an ever-widening and everlasting need for continued improvement. Accountants need to remember that analysts (and other readers) must examine hundreds or thousands of financial statements yearly. Thus accountants have a standing obligation to improve their products. Analysts feel that much remains to be done in the campaign to make more corporate information readily available.[1]

---

[1]It is noteworthy that analysts feel that the state of availability of corporate information in Canada is now at about the same sketchy level as it was in the United States in the early 1920s.

CHAPTER II

THE ANALYST'S VIEWPOINT IN PERSPECTIVE

Professional financial analysts are probably the most avid consumers of published financial information. It is evident that accountants have a primary obligation to consider analysts' wants and needs, just as any producer must consider the wants and needs of his customers. This chapter will attempt to delineate the position of the analyst as a consumer of the products of the accountant.

The position of the analyst with respect to financial reporting is concisely summarized as follows:

> Probably no great percentage of those who read financial statements can make an intelligent forecast irrespective of how complete the information may be, but there are enough who can; and they have sufficient stake in corporate securities so that the information should be published.[1]

Decision-making or decision-influencing, with its inherent crystal-ball gazing, is the ultimate task of the analyst. William Vatter's observations about decisions are directly applicable to the analyst's duties: "It is easier to make a decision with fewer factors to judge, and the answer is likely to be a better one, if the process of measurement is applied as far as it can be, to reduce the amount of guesswork, even though there must always be some guessing done."[2]

---

[1]Carman G. Blough, "Accounting Reports and Their Meaning to the Public," Journal of Accountancy, LXVIII, No. 3 (September, 1939), 163.

[2]William J. Vatter, Managerial Accounting (New York: Prentice-Hall, Inc., 1950), p. 362.

Financial statements provide some of the many components of the tool-box of the analyst.[1] In order to perform efficiently the analyst must be equipped with those tools which aid him in finishing a job as quickly and thoroughly as possible.[2] He needs more than highly condensed statements marked by vague terminology and minimum, sketchy explanations.

One of the major concerns of analysts is future earning power and "value."[3] But such notions are conjectural and

---

[1] For an excellent discussion of elements in investment analysis (quantitative and qualitative) see B. Graham and D. Dodd, Security Analysis (3rd ed.; New York: McGraw-Hill Book Co., Inc., 1951), pp. 68-76.

[2] Jerome N. Frank, as Chairman of the S.E.C., "Accounting for Investors," Journal of Accountancy, LXVIII, No. 5 (November, 1939), 302, observed: "It is a function of the financial statements also to supply basic material for making an educated guess. Precisely because the unknowables are many, all the knowables should within reason be thoroughly explained and fairly and fully disclosed."

[3] Ralph Badger and Harry Guthmann, Investment Principles and Practices (4th ed.; New York: Prentice-Hall, Inc., 1951), p. 246, comment: "It has been our contention that the market value of common stocks is a function of earnings available and of the risk factors involved in the industry and in the concern itself."

Jerome N. Frank, op. cit., p. 299, observed: "The ultimately controlling fact affecting the investor . . . is nothing more or less than the reasonably prospective net earning power. . . . Value, thus conceived, is capitalized earning power."

Maurice Kaplan and Daniel Reaugh, "Accounting Reports to Stockholders, and the S.E.C.," Accounting Review, XIV, No. 3 (September, 1939), 206, commented: "Accountants and investment analysts today are agreed that the income statement is much more significant and informative to the investor than the balance sheet. It is of cardinal importance, because the 'value' of a business depends, not on the historical costs incurred in the process of building it up, but upon its earning capacity."

uncertain. Yet the uncertainty should be reduced even though it cannot be removed. Intelligent thinking about the future should be based upon probabilities, not upon tea leaves or astrology. A practicing analyst observed: "The problem of the investor is to appraise the value of specific securities . . . the successful investor is primarily a student of operating results, which should be revealed in the income statement."[1]

Thus the accountant furnishes part of the raw materials for the investor's judgment. The materials that are made available should be as pure as possible, but the analyst's judgment cannot consist wholly of those materials, nor can the accountant be asked to perform the duties of the security analyst.

To summarize, one of the purposes of financial statements is to supply substantive raw material which will be combined with other investment factors into a reasoned judgment concerning the prospects of an enterprise. Because the unknown aspects with regard to a decision at hand are myriad, all the known aspects should within reason be thoroughly described and fairly and completely disclosed. For the most part this writer feels wholeheartedly that in matters of this kind accountants should consider analysts as they <u>are</u> and not as they <u>should be</u> (in the minds of accountants).

---

[1]Paul L. Morrison, "The Interest of the Investor in Accounting Principles," <u>Accounting Review</u>, XII, No. 1 (March, 1937), 38-39. Later (p. 39) Morrison says: "As we have stated, the intelligent investor is interested fundamentally in the earning power. . . . This involves forecasting or budgeting because earning power involves the future."

Committee on Corporate Information

The National Federation of Financial Analysts Societies is deeply interested in this problem of corporate information. In 1948 a Committee on Corporate Information was created by the Federation "to act as a focal point of contact between the corporation and the analyst in problems arising in this field. . . . The Committee will act as a clearinghouse for suggestions and complaints on deficiencies in reporting from all analysts and will bring these suggestions to the attention of corporation officials."[1] The Committee represents the analysts' point of view on the subject as distinguished from that of the accountant, government official or corporate manager.[2]

It is noteworthy that the analysts have approached this problem from an individual industry point of view. This approach again reflects the analysts' desires (which were mentioned again and again to this writer) for more uniformity and more disclosure in order to facilitate comparison. So far studies of the chemical, paper, banking, oil and electrical utility industries have been completed. Studies-in-process include the insurance, drug, merchandising and aircraft-manufacturing industries.[3]

In all of its reports and in the articles of its members the Committee has stressed the point that corporate management should give more and more weight to the importance placed by the financial community on the comparison of similar enterprises and,

---

[1]Committee on Corporate Information, "Initial Report," The Analysts Journal, X, No. 1 (February, 1954), 51.

[2]E. Linwood Savage, Jr., "Conclusions Regarding Annual Reports," The Analysts Journal, X, No. 1 (February, 1954), 51.

[3]Ibid., p. 50.

"in co-operation with other managements within an industry, should see to it that financial figures are comparable or that the necessary supplementary information is supplied so that the analyst can make them comparable."[1]

One of the principal tasks of the analyst consists of comparison. He compares the characteristics of different industries and relates industries to their economic environments. He compares the current and past performance of companies within the industries themselves.[2]

It follows, therefore, that financial information supplied by accountants should be oriented toward facilitating comparisons. The following specific factors are the ones which need scrutiny in judging reporting practice in this regard: consistency of presentation, clarity, basis of consolidation, income statement details, handling of non-recurring items, uniformity, price level adjustments, and "valuation" techniques. These factors will be appraised in detail in the next six chapters.

Comparability and Disclosure

Comparison and disclosure are obviously intertwined. The analyst cannot readily compare inter-year and/or inter-company items if (a) he does not comprehend the assumptions underlying the valuation of the items; (b) he does not know of changes in accounting policies through time; (c) he does not know the quantitative

---

[1]Ibid

[2]See Ralph R. Pickett and Marshall D. Ketchum, Investment Principles and Policy (New York: Harper and Bros., 1954), chap. viii, pp. 164-165, 168-174, 175-176, et passim.
Also see John H. Prime, Investment Analysis (New York: Prentice-Hall, Inc., 1952), pp. 290-291, 293-294, et passim.

impact of changes in accounting policies upon the financial statements at hand; (d) he does not know of any unusual items important enough to distort comparisons; and (e) he does not know of significant matters (important price level effects) which are buried in large unexplained items or omitted altogether. Probably a succinct, meaningful standard to be met would be as follows: Any information should be disclosed which would significantly affect comparisons between years and/or between similar firms.[1]

Analysts as a group are decidedly more discontented with the absence of comparability and disclosure with reference to income statements rather than balance sheets. They are vitally concerned with future earning power. They feel that many of the quantitative clues can be found in the income statements. They emphasize "normal operating income" but give due weight to all important classifications in the income statement.[2] Able accountants are often inclined to scoff at the tendency to give too much weight to normal earning power.[3] They cry to the effect that the

---

[1] Blough, op. cit., p. 163.

[2] This writer found that the analysts themselves say that the earnings per share figure is extremely significant but still their own thinking and written analyses do not give nearly the weight to the earnings per share figure which one might imagine. Rather, the written analyses are much more thorough, with decided emphasis on a source and application of funds approach to the income statement (see Chapter VIII). Thus net earnings per share is an important factor in analysis; yet, if one judges by their written analyses, its importance has been woefully overemphasized by analysts themselves. See Chapter VI for a more detailed presentation of the analysts' emphasis upon "normal" earnings.

[3] See H.C. Greer and E.B. Wilcox, "The Case Against Price Level Adjustments in Income Determination," Journal of Accountancy, XC, No. 6 (December, 1950), 500.

measurement of income is an intricate task which is peppered with pitfalls. The matching of costs against revenue demands opinions, judgments, and estimates which are often difficult to support by "facts." Such thought-provoking questions as depreciation estimates, bad debts, contingent liabilities, carrying values of inventories and fixed assets, and the accuracy of amortization of deferred charges are inherently uncertain. Even original "cost" is far from being a Gibraltar.

Granted, income determination is a Gargantuan job. But it is the job of the accountant. And, at least for the present, he cannot solve the problem by assuming it away or by saying that the net income notion is nonsense and should be scrapped. Rather, he must face up to the task of the moment. It is his duty to inform the reader of his statement of all his major assumptions and to furnish adequate supplementary information. In this way, if the reader differs with the assumptions, or if he is comparing A Company's income statement with B Company's statement (which was made under different assumptions), the reader is equipped to conduct a more meaningful comparison.

It seems almost ludicrous that so often financial statements are displayed as if they were infallible portrayals of dynamics and uncertainties of a throbbing business enterprise. Picture them--balances precisely drawn; classifications neatly indented; figures to the nearest penny; and "net worth" and "net income" basking in immutable fashion. And then accountants are chagrined at the misinterpretations of the figures by the financial press, by union leaders, and by stockholders! Something should be done to improve this situation. That "something" is summarized by one word, "disclosure." Use of the words, "judgment" and "opinion," sprinkled more generously over the financial statements, along with the divulging of more information, would be steps in a fruitful direction.

Management and Disclosure

The argument as to whether disclosure is the primary responsibility either of managers or the accountants who serve them is not considered to be relevant here. What is relevant is that public and private accountants should take it upon themselves to increase disclosure wherever possible and in whatever manner seems propitious.

The growing social consciousness of many managers, especially those of the larger firms, may be one of the contributing factors toward greater disclosure in future years. But analysts complain that many managers still often balk at disclosing operating details of their firm.[1] Managers have many misgivings (sometimes warranted and sometimes not).[2] They want to keep details

---

[1]Jeremy C. Jenks, "The Financial Community's Role in Stockholder Relations," The Analysts Journal, IV, No. 4 (December, 1948), 37, portrays the typical analyst's reaction to "secretive" firms as follows: ". . . the investment adviser is likely to answer the inquiries of clients concerning a particular company: 'It is reported to be a good company, but it is not easy to get up-to-date information on it. Therefore, it probably would be better for you to buy the security of another company instead which can be followed closely. . . .' Well-informed corporate executives recognize the important fact that their company is competing every day with at least twenty-five hundred other prosperous well-managed companies in the United States for public attention and support. It, therefore, behooves them to use modern businesslike methods in handling their relationships with the financial community."

[2]Committee on Corporate Information, "Second Annual Report," The Analysts Journal, VI, No. 2 (May, 1950), 139, criticizes management as follows:

"The efforts of the committee have not been without

from competitors, from the anti-trusters, from other government agencies, from their own employees, from their customers, from their stockholders. Their reasons are many and varied. They often fear governmental probing into their affairs and hesitate to invite it by disclosing any more information than is absolutely necessary. They often guard operating details because of possible unfavorable impacts upon labor relations. They often do not want their internal operating and financial policies too closely inspected by stockholders.[1] They often fear the possible displeasure of their customers if certain mark-ups and other policies were known. They often state that it would not be proper to give information to a limited group of stockholders without releasing it to all stockholders.

---

disappointments. Some managements have shown a marked disinterest in requests for additional information. It appears that company officials have a tendency to hide behind certain stock cliches when they are seeking excuses for not making available more information for stockholders and financial analysts. These excuses follow the same general form, as follows:

1. The release of such information would hurt their competitive position.
2. Data requested is misleading.
3. It would not be proper to give such information to a limited group of stockholders without releasing it to all stockholders.

"The committee feels that these excuses are usually invalid for most types of information, and it will continue to combat vigorously such objections wherever they are pursued by corporation officials."

[1] Benjamin Graham, "Financial Statements from the Viewpoint of the Financial Analyst," New York Certified Public Accountant, XV, No. 5 (May, 1945), 239, comments: "Many years ago I raised an interesting question on this point. What liability did the corporation's officials have for failure to show to their stockholders how much depreciation they took on the tax return, in order to enable the individual stockholder to make up his own mind as to whether the amount shown on the income account was sufficient? Well, up to recently the lawyers seemed to advise the officers that they were on firm ground in not revealing these facts; but I notice more and more a tendency to give all the facts in the financial statements, probably for fear of possible liability."

Many executives reveal the wanted details to inquiring analysts but do not disclose them in published reports. This discriminatory attitude is not commendable. The "privileged few" attitude was one of the major criticisms of management in the 1920s.[1] Analysts favor the publishing of all details for all to use because of the inconvenience and expense of obtaining this information in other ways.

Analysts are often justifiably disturbed by managerial reluctance to publish certain significant figures. Analysts are reasonable men. For the most part they do not expect annual reports to contain the sweeping details found in the company 10-K reports which are filed with the Securities and Exchange Commission. But skilled analysts are disturbed by the delay and extra effort required in order to get significant figures which can be found in 10-K reports or obtained through other less convenient means.[2]

Fundamentally, it must be remembered that financial statements submitted to stockholders are reports to those with a proprietary interest in the firm. By using this perspective the issues of disclosure become less difficult to settle.[3]

---

[1]See Carl B. Robbins, "Business Secrets," Accounting Review, IV, No. 2 (June, 1929), 65-66.

[2]M.C. Kaplan and Daniel M. Reaugh, op. cit., p. 204, point to the problem of inconvenience as follows: "Reports filed with the Commission, except where regarded as confidential, are available in Washington to the public either by personal examination or by paying the cost of duplication. Except for institutional or other substantial investors, who before the Exchange Act often managed to get the information anyway, such cost is likely to be prohibitive, and the effort to obtain it is so great that only the most energetic investor will bestir himself." The national securities exchanges also are required to keep the registration statements and annual 10-K reports of issuers open for public inspection.

[3]B. Graham and D. Dodd, op. cit., p. 67, refer to this

Confidential Information

What information is "confidential?" Through the years this term has tended to become narrower in scope as managers of many major firms have adopted more liberal attitudes.[1] "Trade secrets" and "competitive reasons" are no longer felt to be the crutches which they were formerly. Most of the analysts interviewed felt that competitors are closely acquainted with the what, how, and why of the operations of their rivals. Therefore, the analyst feels that stockholders should rightfully share information readily available to other firms in the industry. Furthermore, the fact that so many companies (i.e., Monsanto, Eastman Kodak, Borden, Allied Stores) do publish important details of their operations would seem to yield adequate reply to "secrecy" reasons.

Realistically speaking, there is much more exchange of information among competitors than executives are willing to admit.[2]

---

point as follows:

"It must never be forgotten that a stockholder is an owner of the business and an employer of its officers. He is entitled not only to ask legitimate questions but also to have them answered, unless there is some persuasive reason to the contrary.

"Insufficient attention has been paid to this all-important point. . . .

"This is particularly true when the information asked for is no more than that which is regularly published by other companies in the same field."

[1]For example, Harry G. Guthmann, Analysis of Financial Statements (4th ed.; New York: Prentice-Hall, Inc., 1953), pp. 16-17, refers to a 1929 advertisement of General Motors which begins, "In recent years there has developed an increasing tendency on the part of forward-looking corporations to take their stockholders and the public more fully into their confidence." The advertisement went on to relate how General Motors keeps interested parties informed through quarterly financial statements and monthly news releases with respect to total sales of automobiles.

[2]Jeremy C. Jenks, op. cit., p. 39, comments: "Part of

For example, John E. Bierwirth, President, National Distillers Products Corporation, has stated: "We swap research information, sales figures and other data with other firms, such as Union Carbide and du Pont, whenever we think it is advantageous to both companies."[1]

The subcommittee on Annual Reports of Drug Companies of the Committee on Corporate Information of the National Federation of Financial Analysts had the following comments:

> Much more information could be published without fear of damage to competitive position. Each of the drug companies has a lot of knowledge as to what its competitors are doing, therefore, a more complete sales breakdown than is provided by the majority could be given to stockholders. Information regarding manufacturing costs is more debatable, but here again competitors have a good general idea and it is probable that more information than is now being provided could be safely presented. The basis of this view is that where there is keen competition in a product, the competing companies watch each other very closely. There is much exchange of scientific information between the laboratories of the drug houses. The technicians attend conventions and meetings together and visit socially. In this regard they are very much like security analysts.[2]

On the other hand, there are certainly instances where the interests of the stockholders might best be served by

---

the difficulty has been that some of the information that corporation officers classify as confidential is in no sense of the word information that should not be made public or that is not available from other sources. A few companies still refuse to release sales figures: for example, on the ground that this knowledge if available to competitors would hurt the position of their business. Actual experience shows that detailed data concerning sales and operations, even including detailed breakdowns of operating figures, can generally be released without any repercussions on a company's trade position."

[1]John E. Bierwirth, "A Corporate Financial History," speech to The Forum on Finance, New York City, August 25, 1954.

[2]Subcommittee on Annual Reports of Drug Companies, Committee on Corporate Information, National Federation of Financial Analysts Societies, "Suggestions for the Improvement of Drug Company Annual Reports," unpublished mimeographed report, June 8, 1954, p. 2.

withholding financial information. It seems reasonable to assume that most stockholders feel that corporate executives' first responsibility is to maximize profits (and thus increase dividends and enhance the market value of the company stock).[1] If disclosure of information will deter the firm from this objective, it would seem that withholding is justified. However, when doubt arises as to publication, the information should be revealed. The stockholder is entitled to know what is going on. The history of Talon, Inc., is an example in this regard:

> Prior to 1944, Talon had never published a report of any kind. However, there was a reason for not publishing information. Talon was the first in its field--that of making slide fasteners or zippers. It developed the zipper and the means for making it, then developed the markets. It had a very lucrative business and consequently was not interested in openly inviting competition. Had we published financial information in the 1930s, we would have invited competition to come in earlier than it actually did, which would have seriously impaired the growth of our company. Fortunately, too, the number of stockholders was not large.
>
> By 1944, this picture had changed. The zipper was no longer a novelty item; it was an accepted commodity. Competition was an important factor in the various markets. The holdings of some of the larger stockholders, either because of death or other reasons, had been reduced and the number of stockholders more than tripled. In 1944 the management recognized its responsibility to keep its growing number of stockholders informed and commenced the publication of an annual report.[2]

---

[1]Many economists and others feel that profit maximization is not always the most important objective of corporate activity. Growth for growth's sake, power for power's sake, and "reasonable" profits have also been cited as objectives. See Joel Dean, Managerial Economics (New York: Prentice-Hall, Inc., 1951), pp. 28-39.

[2]J.E. Turner, "A Treasurer Looks at His Own Annual Report," Journal of Accountancy, XCII, No. 2 (August, 1951), 225.

What To Do About It

Greater disclosure can be one of the contributing factors toward the improvement of the analyst's tools.[1] Managers and boards of directors must become more acutely aware of their obligations in this area.[2] What can the accountants do to help? The answer is probably two-fold.

First, the independent public accountant can be of significant service.[3] One way of viewing the accountant's opportunity in this connection is:

> It is impossible now to escape the social implications of large-scale business enterprise. Its affairs are matters of public, as well as private concern. Public accounting must, therefore, assume a full responsibility for the preparation of sound and informative reports on the operations of business, or await the time when the alternative of rigid governmental control of such matters will become an established fact.[4]

---

[1]Committee on Corporate Information, op. cit., p. 79, has the following apt comment: "The problem is not confined solely to disclosure of information, but embraces adequacy, timeliness, and quality of information--method and form of reports--and, in fact, all contacts between analysts and corporations."

[2]Albert I. Stiles, "Corporate Management," The Analysts Journal, III, No. 3 (September, 1947), 10-13, is particularly critical of boards of directors with respect to this problem. He believes that corporate directors as a class have not been fully alive to their responsibilities.

[3]Study Group on Business Income, Changing Concepts of Business Income (New York: Macmillan Co., 1952), p. 107, comments: "The independent accountant should continue to recognize an obligation to pass upon the appropriateness of the methods employed and the fairness of the manner of their application in determining the income reported, and should assume a similar responsibility in respect to the supplementary information which forms a part of the material on which he passes."

[4]Roy A. Foulke, Practical Financial Statement Analysis (New York: McGraw-Hill Book Co., Inc., 1950), p. 605.

Even if one tries hard to look at it another way, however, the substance of the annual report is the responsibility of management. Auditors cannot easily thrust their notions about financial reporting upon executives. An auditor can withhold certification of financial statements, if they are misleading because of lack of disclosure. Sometimes deficient disclosure may be commented upon by the accountant in his certificate. But in such cases any information which is contained in the certificate could be, by somewhat stronger inducement, included in the statements or footnotes themselves.

Public accountants are faced with difficult decisions in these matters. But if they remember that stockholders deserve adequate information, auditors will have a compelling principle in determining their own courses of action. When management does not make disclosures which seem to be significant--at least to some degree, the public accountant can use his persuasive powers plus the weapon of the qualified or withheld certificate in order to stir management toward further disclosure. More frequent examinations of conscience on the part of public accountants with respect to this problem are in order.

Second, the chief accounting officer (usually the controller) of the firm should use his influence also to improve disclosure.[1] The controller has intimate knowledge of his

---

[1]Earle C. King, "The Corporate Controller's Relation to the Securities and Exchange Commission." The Controller, XVIII, No. 12, 541-42, cites the following remarks, made by Commissioner Robert E. Healy, of the S.E.C., on May 15, 1939, in an address before the Midwestern Conference of the Controllers Institute:

"What we need, it seems to me is a return to the recognition that the primary responsibility for proper accounting rests on the corporate management in the person of the controller. Whether the books are audited or not, the stockholder has a right

company's accounting policies and problems. The investor has a special interest in the boundaries of the controller's responsibility and authority. If the controller is armed with an ample amount of responsibility and independence, the value of his services to the management and stockholders is enhanced. He will be better equipped to structure the company accounting with the objective of insuring the complete documentation and reporting of the facts, judgments, opinions and estimates with respect to the enterprise's activities.

Summary

Analysts are major consumers of financial information. As investors or advisers to investors, they are entitled to adequate disclosure of corporate information in order that they might be better able to make intelligent decisions. They need details, especially with respect to income statement items, in order to facilitate comparisons.

Time-worn reasons for withholding financial information _generally_ are no longer compelling. Because most of the data can be obtained anyway, more comprehensive disclosure is warranted in annual reporting. In this way all investors will rank

---

to look to the corporation's own accounting system for an adequate, intelligible and honest reporting of its affairs. Unless in its daily bookkeeping the corporation recognizes a responsibility to stockholders and investors, the most conscientious audits lose much of their meaning."

King, chief accountant for the S.E.C., then comments: "Inasmuch as the primary responsibility for proper accounting does rest on corporate management and, more specifically, on the controller, it follows that the controller must have complete knowledge, and be expert in the application of the principles underlying the recording and reporting of financial transactions. . . .

"I feel that as a body you have not been as forceful in making your views known as your position in the accounting profession warrants. This is especially true, I think, with respect to the development of uniform principles of accounting."

abreast as far as availability of significant financial information is concerned.

Public accountants and controllers have an obligation to do all that is within reason to persuade management to report more fully about the operations of the firm.

CHAPTER III

ANALYSTS AND QUANTITATIVE DATA

This chapter is an effort to outline the uses of accounting information by financial analysts. This presentation is primarily based upon the writer's scrutiny of 123 written analysts' reports on companies and upon the information and opinions garnered from interviews with 51 analysts.

Generalizations which are based upon the above investigation are believed to be valid and applicable to any appraisal of accounting. However, although their approaches are similar, what financial analysts actually do is not uniform. Practice is marked (a) by varying degrees of emphasis on various investment factors; (b) by the over-all investment policy of the chief investment officers involved; (c) by the time that is devoted to studies of specific companies; and (d) by the competence of the analysts themselves. Thus this chapter serves as a frame of reference for the appraisal of accounting and reporting practice that is found in the following chapters. It does not intend to invade the impossible realm of trying to determine the deciding factors in investment decision-making. Rather it attempts to describe the normal everyday uses of accounting information by security analysts. Herein is the emphasis. Other factors, while often overwhelmingly important in investment decisions, are necessarily avoided in order to keep this study within manageable limits.

Sources of Financial Data

There is widespread agreement among security analysts that the company annual report serves as the springboard for their periodic (usually annual) review of a company of interest.[1] Although the annual report is not always the most important source of information, in terms of universal usage it belongs in first place among the sources.[2] Analysts also regard personal interviews and contacts with company officers as being extremely valuable. Many investment organizations do a great deal of company visiting, while others tend to minimize this type of investigation. Other important sources of information include exchanges of information among fellow analysts, prospectuses, statistical services, annual Form 10-K reports to the Securities and Exchange Commission, and research services offered by organizations such as Argus Research, Inc., Wainwright and Co., and Duff, Anderson and Clark.

A candid appraisal of the abilities of management is an essential part of most written analyses. Usually the top-ranking people in the investment organization either know key executives

---

[1] E. Linwood Savage, Jr., "Conclusions Regarding Annual Reports," The Analysts Journal, X, No. 1 (February, 1954), 51, states "We believe that the annual report should be regarded by corporate management as the primary source of information for stockholders regarding the current status and prospects of their companies."

[2] Oscar M. Miller, "Retrogression in Annual Reports to Stockholders?" Analysts Journal, I, No. 1 (January, 1945), 49, observes: "Despite the advent of the S.E.C., the annual corporation report is still the basic tool used by the security analyst. The publication of the corporate report usually preceeds the S.E.C. release by weeks or months, and, in addition, it is readily available in financial libraries. More important, however, the president's letter accompanying the financial statements often does, and always should, give supplementary information relating to the operation of business. This the standardized S.E.C. report cannot present."

in the firm being studied or they (or the analyst himself) often obtain personal interviews with company executives in order to secure important information about such things as product development, competitive position, changes in policy, and data on research, sales, and capital expansion. Personal interviews also yield clues with regard to the attitudes and personalities of the members of the management team. These impressions are recorded in the analyst's report. An excerpt from an analyst's report on the Burroughs Corporation is an example of the types of opinions offered:

> The aggressiveness of the new management team has already been noted. We have had a . . . relationship with the company for many years and (an investment official) appraises the group as follows:
>
> "John Coleman was elected President . . . in 1946. Previously the company had been like Packard and Parke Davis in Detroit in that it had old, conservative nonprogressive management content to more or less rest on a strong financial condition and not depend on alert aggressive progress. Under Coleman, and his top Vice President Eppert, both of whom came up through sales, the company has turned into a dynamic group who are aggressively after new products and new markets. Tiffany, Financial Vice President, whom we see frequently, impresses me as an able man. Eppert has been a friend of (another investment official) for many years and (another investment official) regards him highly.
>
> "I think this is one of the most alert and aggressive crowds on whom we call in Detroit."[1]

Many analysts say they give great weight to the value of personal interviews with company officials. Investment people spend a good deal of time, effort, and money in this task. While admitting that personal interviews are valuable and necessary, one may still wonder about the efficiency of this method of

---

[1]For another example of these types of opinions see the excerpt from an analysis of the Hazel-Atlas Glass Company in Chapter VII.

gathering corporate information.[1] Would not efforts in this direction be lessened if more information were readily available in published annual reports?

Comparison

As mentioned previously, the analyst's task is one of comparison--comparison of changing economic conditions through time, comparison of industries, comparison of similar firms within industries and comparison of specific company financial data

---

[1]Alex Bozic, "Patterns of Investment Research," The Analysts Journal, V, No. 2 (May, 1949), 34-35, offers an interesting discussion of the merits of "libraries and files" vs field trips in investment research. He seems to favor the former and is wary of the value of the latter. He comments: "In theory both methods are supposed to be part and parcel of the same operation; they are supposed to be complementary. But in practice too often the two methods are at odds. The analyst in his office animates information available from his files and libraries, makes the record speak. The personal contact man, on the other hand, endeavors to make the corporation management do the talking. The abstract factor in the first method and the human factor in the second method frequently cause their findings and conclusions on the same subject to be controversial, often skeptical in one case and optimistic in the second.

"In many investment organizations the persuasion is quite common, particularly in prosperous times, that investment research by personal contact is worth the price and the risk. . . . The danger is for the contact man to make the home trip just as infected with optimism as the people he talked to. . . .

"It is not unusual for important financial transactions involving millions of dollars of new corporate funds to be closed on the strength of a walk through the plant and engineering department of the borrower and to pass over the cool analytical approach in the home office of the lender.

"The contact man, scouting for information, whether he knows it or not is exposed to a multitude of insidious factors, some of them belonging to the nature and personality of the executives he interviews. . . . By contrast, working within the walls of his office, the investment research worker is left to his counsel in the matter of selecting and lining up his source material, in the weighing of the positives and the negatives. He makes it a practice of comparing several corporations operating in the same field and under similar circumstances and appraises their performance through operating and financial statements and other statistical yardsticks. He can see the trees and the forest, and he can measure many times before he cuts, protected from any catalytic influences of outside personalities."

through the years.[1] The writer has never seen an analyst's report which does not include comparative data.[2] Often the comparisons span ten years, and in one case rose to twenty-three years. Five to ten year summaries of financial data are common in these analyses.

The committee on Corporate Information of the National Federation of Financial Analysts Societies has formally requested more widespread use of comparative figures as follows: "The Committee further recommends to corporations that five year or longer summaries of financial data be included in annual reports. . . ."[3]

E. Linwood Savage, Jr., chairman of the Committee on Corporate Information, feels that corporate management should give more consideration to the importance placed by security analysts on the comparison of similar companies.[4] Savage also states: ". . . it would be well to confirm what seems obvious to

---

[1]Benjamin Graham, "Financial Statements from the Viewpoint of the Financial Analyst," New York Certified Public Accountant, XV, No. 5 (May, 1945), 237, comments: "You cannot make an investment in a vacuum; and investing in relation to the position of one company, taken by itself, is practically investing in a vacuum."

[2]Lincoln W. Hall, "Security Analysis from the Point of View of a Trust Company," The Analysts Journal, IX, No. 2 (May, 1953), 123, observes: "No individual security, whether it is a common stock, preferred stock, or bond, is studied all by itself or in a vacuum. The individual security must be related to the capital structure of the company, the company to its industry, and the industry to the economic conditions of the country."

[3]Committee on Corporate Information, "Fourth Annual Report," The Analysts Journal, VIII, No. 4 (August, 1952), 216.

[4]E. Linwood Savage, Jr., "Conclusions Regarding Annual Reports," The Analysts Journal, X, No. 1 (February, 1954), 52.

most of us that two-year comparative statements are essential and that five or ten-year summaries of financial data, including cash-flow statements, are very helpful to analysts."[1]

The Committee on Corporate Information has been studying specific industries and has constantly sought more uniformity in reporting in order to facilitate comparisons.[2] This is one of the primary reasons why the Committee studies individual industries rather than corporate reporting in general.

The mountain (sometimes foothill) of figures made available to analysts is invariably picked over and recast to fit the analyst's and his readers' needs or purposes. Much of the data which is wanted by the analyst is sifted from the readily available company annual report.[3] But unfortunately, much of the data must be secured elsewhere. As already mentioned, analysts also secure needed information (a) from fellow analysts; (b) from the inefficient and expensive personal interview with company officers; and (c) from subscriptions to the services of investment research organizations that have the necessary contacts for obtaining the desired information.

---

[1] Ibid., p. 53.

[2] Cf. Committee on Corporate Information, Reports of National Committees for 1953 (New York: New York Society of Security Analysts, Inc., 1954), p. 15. Additional plans for more comparative data and more uniformity in reporting can be found in an unpublished mimeographed report dated June 8, 1954, on "Suggestions for the Improvement of Drug Company Annual Reports," p. 3.

[3] Committee on Corporate Information, "Report of the Subcommittee on the Adequacy of the Annual Reports of the Chemical Industry," The Analysts Journal, VI, No. 2 (May, 1950), 68, comments: "The annual report of a chemical company (any company in fact), offers the analyst his first line of attack in examining the condition of a particular company."

Emphasis on Future

What kind of quantitative analysis is found in the written reports of the analysts? The following paragraphs will reflect the pattern that is almost always found, even though the analyst's order of presentation differs as among investment organizations.

As most investment literature indicates, investment analysis is concerned with projecting future performance.[1] Analysts investigate financial data in order to find indicators and trends which might yield clues with respect to potential achievements.[2] Analysts also feel that the quantitative data furnishes concrete evidence which can be used in judging managerial performance. Thus the quality of management, an all-important investment factor, is reflected in the company financial display.[3]

---

[1]Lincoln W. Hall, op. cit., p. 123, observes: "We are really seeking to discover the influences at work that will produce the balance sheets and income statements of the future, and not the ones that we have in front of us at the moment."

[2]The following is a tabular presentation of how one investment organization attempts to estimate key figures five years into the future:

Earnings Projection

Capital Expenditures	Taxes as Per Cent of Net Before Taxes
Depreciation and Amortization	Net after Taxes Per Share
Sales	Working Capital
1. Sales to Gross Plant Ratio	Long-term debt
2. Product Breakdown	Dividends
Net before Taxes	Number of Shares
Per cent of Sales	

[3]One analyst who was interviewed when asked about the factor of management, stated concisely: "Management is judged by financial results."

Income Statement

From the viewpoint of the security analyst the income statement dwarfs the balance sheet in importance. Future earning power is the major consideration. Past earnings performance is dissected in order to delineate trends. The analyst is not nearly as "single-figure" minded (earnings per share) as he leads people to believe by his remarks and articles. Instead the analyst begins with the sales figures and methodically weaves through the remainder of the statement. Besides sales the major components which command attention are cost of goods sold, research, long-term rentals, depreciation charges, non-recurring items, net "operating" income, income taxes, and net income.

Sales

Once a major criticism, but one that now applies mainly to "over-the-counter" companies, is the deliberate omission of sales figures in the income statement.[1] The lack of gross revenue figures "effectively bars the analyst from ascertaining most of the important quantitative factors on which security values hinge."[2] Some firms have evidently guarded the sales figure because their profit margins are so wide as to border on embarrassment if known to customers or labor unions.[3] Other firms

---

[1]Research Department, American Institute of Accountants, Accounting Trends and Techniques, 1953 edition (New York: American Institute of Accountants, 1953), p. 171, points out that forty firms out of 600 surveyed did not reveal sales in their income statements.

[2]J.M. Galanis, "Shortcomings of Financial Statements from the Security Analyst's Viewpoint," The Analysts Journal, III, No. 4 (November, 1947).

[3]Among the large companies which still withhold sales figures in annual reporting are Coca-Cola, Inc.; The Parker Pen Company; The Gruen Watch Co.; Merchant Calculators, Inc.; and The Sherwin-Williams Company.

say that they fear vulnerability to competition.[1] But unusually wide margins may not necessarily mean vulnerability to new competition; traditionally wide margins have long been shown in the cigarette, precision instrument, and drug fields.

The analysts' interest in sales figures extends beyond the annual total revenue. For comparative purposes they are intensely interested in quarterly sales figures. This year (1954) the Securities and Exchange Commission removed its requirement that all corporations under its jurisdiction publish quarterly sales figures. Analysts' reactions were immediate and intense.[2] The restoration of this S.E.C. requirement is now one of the primary goals of the Committee on Corporate Information of the National Federation of Financial Analysts Societies.[3]

Annual lump-sum sales figures are no longer regarded as being adequate disclosure by the discriminating analysts. The multi-product firms of today's business environment necessitate the securing or estimating of breakdowns of sales by divisions, by product, by geographical distribution and/or by consuming industry.[4] Especially important in this area is the per cent of

---

[1]J.E. Turner, "A Treasurer Looks at His Own Annual Report," Journal of Accountancy, XCII, No. 2 (August, 1951), 225, says that Talon, Inc., (zipper manufacturers) did not disclose information in its early years because it "was not interested in openly inviting competition."

[2]Chicago American (August 5, 1954), p. 28.

[3]Personal interview with Jeremy C. Jenks, Member of Committee on Corporate Information, September 9, 1954.

[4]The rails and utilities under regulation are required to furnish breakdowns of sales. Monsanto shows a breakdown by product and by consuming industry. Eastman Kodak in pictorial form gives detailed figures for both sales (by product) and costs. Marquette Cement provides a two-year comparative table of

sales coming from foreign markets.

The tendency to divide sales into its major components is already evident in a few scattered annual reports. As business becomes more complicated and diversified, such breakdowns are an aid to the comprehension of the nature of a company. Savage comments:

> No specific preference for a particular types of breakdown can be given for annual reports in general--it all depends. We suggest that management try to provide us with the type of breakdown that will be most helpful to us in our job of appraising the possible effects of outside developments on individual companies. It is important for us to know, for example, that less than 16 per cent of Eastman Kodak's sales are cellulose fiber, in estimating the effect of the current slump in the textile industry on that company's earnings.[1]

Analysts always attempt to estimate such sales breakdowns in their written reports.[2] With such information analysts can

---

sales and cost details. Allied Stores gives quarterly figures for a five-year period. Borden reveals a breakdown by divisions. General Motors does not show amounts except to denote civilian and defense totals, but at least it lists the number of cars sold by make.

[1]Savage, op. cit., p. 53.

[2]The following excerpts from an analytical report on the E.I. du Pont de Nemours and Company illustrate the exhaustive extent of analysts' sales breakdowns:

"As the largest chemical company in the world, du Pont's operations straddle the entire fields of organic and inorganic chemistry. . . . Its business is necessarily subject to the ups and downs of general chemical operations, but du Pont concentrates its efforts in chemicals with higher than average profit margins, which require not only introducing new chemicals but also having the decisiveness of abandoning items which develop lower than average profit margins. In carrying out this policy, du Pont in 1953 discontinued three activities--alcohol by fermentation, lithopone pigments, and aromatics for cosmetics, etc. . . .

"In analyzing du Pont, one can isolate some of the Company's major activities and determine the position of du Pont in individual fields, making possible an estimate of the contribution of the particular chemicals to total sales and then determine the outlook in 1954 for the respective activity. . . .

"These sales estimates are approximations assuming a

then better compare trends within companies and among and between the breakdowns of the firm's principal competitors.

The condensing of all operating revenues into a single figure, where the total includes royalty and licensee income, resale items, and important miscellaneous income items can be definitely misleading when the company is compared with others in the same industry. For example, products purchased for resale by a manufacturing company are normally expected to entail narrower margins of profit. Where such resale items comprise a considerable portion of sales, the over-all profit margin may be considerably smaller than for other companies in the same field that have little or no resale business.[1]

Finally, the analyst desires that any material amounts of revenue from dividends, interest, licenses, and royalties be segregated because this type of revenue has frequently tended to evaporate (i.e., patents expire and interest rates drop).

<u>Cost of Goods Sold and Gross Margin</u>

"Cost of goods sold," as used in accounting, is an artificial concept which includes only the "purchase" costs (in cases

---

total sales volume of $1.77 million and present prices. However, where some price cuts seem inevitable or where capacity operations may not be reached, we have lowered somewhat the sales figure. Some of these estimates are quite accurate and are based upon officially announced capacities or plans; others are estimated from industry sources and may be reasonably close but in some cases may be wide of the mark and even somewhat arbitrary. Some of these estimates may be too high and others equally too low. Our purpose is to give a working hypothesis in analyzing the sales and prospects of such a vast company as du Pont. . . . (At this point an estimated breakdown of total sales into twenty-three component parts in dollars per product class is presented.)

"On the following pages we discuss by individual products the position of du Pont and the probable outlook of the particular channels of activity."

[1] Galanis, <u>op. cit</u>., p. 38.

of retailing firms) of goods sold or the "factory" costs (direct material, direct labor, and factory overhead) of producing the goods which have been sold during a period. The excess of sales over "cost of goods sold" is called "gross profit" or gross margin. The accountants who favor the "single-step" income statement feel that the gross margin and all other intermediate "profits" should be eliminated entirely in the presentation of operating results.[1] They feel that all expenses rank abreast as deductions from income, and that there is no "profit" until all expenses have been deducted. For example, with respect to gross margin Paton believes "that the figure has so little significance as to be almost worthless and that, accordingly, it should be given no prominence in the general income report."[2]

Still, one of the "key ratios" which is used by analysts is the gross margin/sales ratio. The current tendencies to lump together the traditional cost of goods sold and operating expenses and/or to present a "single-step" income statement generally are frowned upon by analysts. Gross margin percentages and other operating expense percentages are regarded as being very valuable tools because year-to-year trends can be noted, and comparisons can be made with similar ratios of other companies in the same industry. Galanis maintains that "such comparisons greatly aid in distinguishing the most efficient from the least efficient and high cost enterprises."[3]

---

[1]H.A. Finney and H.E. Miller, Principles of Accounting--Intermediate (4th ed.; New York: Prentice-Hall, Inc., 1951), pp. 135-136, provides an excellent summary of the arguments in favor of a single-step statement.

[2]William A. Paton, "Shortcomings of Present-Day Financial Statements," Journal of Accountancy, LVII, No. 2 (February, 1934), 123.

[3]Galanis, op. cit., p. 39.

Analysts try to obtain separate figures for materials, factory wages, and factory overhead.[1] Again the plea is made because it facilitates year-to-year and company-to-company comparisons.[2]

The nature of the gross margin varies with the character of the cost system adopted by a firm. Caution must be taken in comparing gross margins between companies in the same industry because of the lack of uniformity in the building of the "cost of goods sold" figure.[3] The problem of inventory valuation, discussed in Chapters IV and V, also must be allowed for in making comparisons. However, assuming consistent application in costing methods, year-to-year comparisons of the gross margin performance of a specific company may offer significant clues in investment analysis. Consequently, one wonders if the current trend in accounting practice--toward eliminating "cost of goods sold" and gross margin classifications in the income statement--is desirable. Certainly in light of analysts' uses of such data this trend is in the order of retrogression, because it forces the analyst to speculate as to what types of expenses belong in the "cost of goods sold" category and what types do not.

---

[1]Paul L. Morrison, "Reports to Stockholders," Accounting Review, X, No. 1 (March, 1935), 79. A practicing analyst discusses the value of such figures.

[2]Dwight P. Robinson, Jr., "Accountants' Reports and Audited Accounts from an Investment Analyst's Viewpoint," Journal of Accountancy, LXVII, No. 2 (February, 1939), 80.

[3]Research Department, op. cit., pp. 177-183, shows a startling variety in the classifications and presentations of "cost of goods sold" among the 600 firms surveyed.

Research and Development

The analyst's intense interest in research and development activities typifies his "future-orientation." New products and processes obtain a major share of his attention and a substantial share of the total probing by an analyst beyond the confines of the annual report.

The analysts are interested in alert, progressive management. Research and development activities give clues with regard to managerial efforts to maintain or enhance the competitive position of the firm. Jeremy C. Jenks expresses the analyst's attitudes as follows:

> Perhaps next to a wise management, the most important asset that business can have is a well-organized staff of scientists, searching aggressively for new products and better processes. It is no accident that the most rapidly growing industries are the ones that employ the largest number of technically trained men in their research, engineering, and related departments.[1]

Thorough inspection of research and development outlays includes interest in the total amount, the amount related to sales, the products which show potentialities, and the research program as compared with competitors.

The following passages from an analysis of du Pont de Nemours and Company illustrates the type of thinking that prevails among analysts:

> The experience of du Pont has been to put approximately $3.00 into plant for every $1.00 into research. We estimate that in 1954 research and development expenditure will be $57-60 million--including $10-12 million in basic research. . . .

---

[1]Jeremy C. Jenks, "Projecting Corporate Earnings," The Analysts Journal, IX, No. 1 (February, 1953), 99.

> The du Pont philosophy on research runs along the following lines. Research requires patience, foresight, experience. From 10-20 years may elapse from the first experiment to a commercially profitable product. About one in every 20 projects pays off. The mathematical odds as far as dollars put into research are about 1 in 5; i.e., $1.00 "riding" on a successful product for every $4.00 "down the drain."
>
> Du Pont has a spectrum of scientific opinions through its central research laboratory plus 10 divisional labs plus 3 special labs. Laboratory facilities represent an investment of $66 million. This amounts to about $30,000 for each of its 2,150 technically-trained research workers. At the Experimental Station about 1 out of 3 employees are technically trained and the typical research man or woman is a Ph.D.
>
> Research expenditures were $52 million in 1952 and were approximately $56 million in 1953. The budget is slightly higher for 1954 and we estimate $58-60 million. Research expenditures include pilot plant work but exclude patents and laboratory construction costs. About 20 per cent of the budget is in basic or fundamental research.
>
> The growth of du Pont in its first hundred years ended 1902 was 6 per cent a year. Growth during the past 50 years was 7 1/4 per cent per year. In 1952, 50 per cent of its sales were products unknown or in their commercial infancy 20 years ago. Company estimates that in 1960 about 25 per cent of its sales will be in products virtually unknown today.
>
> Du Pont's record shows that the larger its sales, the higher <u>proportion</u> it <u>can</u> put into research. In other words, in 1952 with sales of $1,600 million, the research budget was $52 million; if du Pont, according to President Greenewalt, had been divided into two companies, with sales of $800 million each, the individual research budget would have been considerably under $26 million. We venture the guess that a dollar invested in research by a group such as du Pont has on the average greater effectiveness than the same dollar put into research by a smaller and less skilled organization.

An excerpt from an analysis of Burroughs Corporation is an example of the comprehensive investigation which analysts conduct with respect to research:

> An aggressive attitude on research and engineering has been adopted in recent years. The biggest step was taken in 1949 when a laboratory was established in Philadelphia and the services of Dr. Irven Travis of the University of Pennsylvania were secured. This laboratory now has a staff in excess of 200 and is being enlarged. Present machines have been redesigned and standardized and the number of models greatly reduced. New mechanical machines have been developed. Research has been pointed toward electronic applications. New developments include: (A two-page detailed summary of progress on various research projects follows.)

The subcommittee on the Chemical Industry of the Committee on Corporate Information of the National Federation of Financial Analysts expressed its dissatisfaction with corporate reporting as follows:

> The greatest inadequacies in this group appear to be the failure to give a breakdown of sales by divisions, sales by industries served, the volume of foreign business, and total research expenditures. The importance of these items for the analyst should be obvious.[1]

The Subcommittee on the Adequacy of Annual Reports of the Paper Industry has made the following sour comment:

> The way in which research was handled was particularly weak. What comments were made were very general in nature. In addition, there was virtually no specific mention made of work being done on the development of new products or new processes that might be forthcoming either to increase sales or to reduce costs. Likewise, there was no mention of the annual expense of the research activities undertaken by the individual companies.[2]

Finally, the Subcommittee on Annual Reports of Drug Companies observes:

> It is highly desirable that the drug companies provide stockholders with more information regarding research than they usually do. Expenditures should not only be stated but also broken down into the different categories as far as possible, i.e., fundamental research, development research, etc. This would permit the reader to form a pretty clear opinion as to how the company is spending its research money. The various areas being explored and the objectives should be discussed. The number of research personnel, including educational background and other qualifications, should be indicated.[3]

---

[1]Committee on Corporate Information, "Chemical Industry," op. cit., p. 68.

[2]Committee on Corporate Information, Subcommittee on the Adequacy of Annual Reports of the Paper Industry, "Third Annual Report," The Analysts Journal, VII, No. 2 (May, 1951), 146.

[3]Subcommittee on Annual Reports of Drug Companies, Committee on Corporate Information, National Federation of Financial Analysts Societies, "Suggestions for the Improvement of Drug Company Annual Reports (unpublished mimeographed report, June 8, 1954, p. 4).

Analysts need research information. Since they seldom get it from annual reports, they rely on a great variety of their other usual sources. But in most cases they do secure it!

Long-Term Rentals

Every analyst interviewed who is concerned with industries where long-term leases are significant expressed his dissatisfaction with corporate information in this respect. The problems of investment analysis involving long-term leases are discussed in detail in Chapter VII. But a summary of the situation is applicable here.

The tendencies toward sale and lease-back of existing facilities and the long-term leasing of new facilities have mushroomed since World War II. Although the retailing industry is the leading example of leasing arrangements, evidence points toward such practices spreading to other industries (leasing of heavy equipment) in much greater volume than before.[1] Therefore the demands upon corporate reporting will tend to become more widespread as leasing practices flourish.

The analysts want and need information about the amount of annual rentals, the terms of the leases, and any other important obligations assumed or guaranteed in connection with leases. Current corporate reporting practices with respect to long-term leases are sorrowfully inadequate. Analysts rightly feel that such commitments are as real and as burdensome as funded debt.[2] Hence reporting the details of such obligations

---

[1]"Equipment Leasing: What's Behind It?" Business Week, No. 138 (September 25, 1954), pp. 41-42.

[2]Two investment analyses of Montgomery Ward revealed

are as important as reporting the details of funded debt.

Depreciation

Analysts feel that depreciation is "something special" because it represents a charge against revenue that does not involve a current outlay of funds. They tend to relate depreciation charges to capital replacements and/or the repayment of long-term debt which arose from prior capital outlays. Thus they think of depreciation amounts as "funds." Whenever depreciation charges are relatively important in the operating picture, they are analyzed with great care. One of the most pressing desires of analysts is to obtain more information with respect to "accelerated amortization" charges which are being made in several industries for fixed assets acquired under certificates of necessity.[1] These charges are often substantial. Consequently the analyst seeks details as to the amount spent on emergency facilities; the total annual amount of accelerated amortization charged; the estimated useful lives of the facilities; and the difference between total depreciation charges including amortization and "normal" depreciation for various classes of facilities.

Many analysts offer analyses on three bases in cases where accelerated amortization is material in amount. First, they present income as reported by the company. Second, they adjust income to a "normal" basis by adding back estimated excess

---

attempts to add rents, maintenance and repairs, and depreciation to Ward's expenses in order to get margins which could be validly compared with Sears.

[1]For example, accelerated amortization is significant in such industries as petroleum, aluminum, chemicals, and aircraft manufacturing.

depreciation.[1] Third, they add back all depreciation charges to the net profit after taxes figure and compare "pseudo-cash" earnings throughout the industry.[2] This matter of accelerated amortization, as well as depreciation, is discussed in much greater detail in Chapters VII and VIII.

Non-Recurring Items

This writer found unanimous agreement in the attitudes of the analysts toward the format of the income statement. The analysts, in varying degrees, attempt to ascertain the normal earning power of the firm. From their point of view, the non-recurring items of the past are irrelevant in regard to projecting future expectations. But adjustments to reported earnings are rarely made in order to determine "true" earning power unless some highly unusual and important charge or credit has been made in the income statement. In other words, the published income statements are generally regarded as the best available reflections of normal earning power and are seldom interpreted as being otherwise. An extended discussion of non-recurring items will be found in Chapter VI.

Net Profit before Taxes and Profit Margins

The most widely used "key ratio" in investment analyses is that of "net operating profit" (before interest, special items,

---

[1]An investment organization treats Dow Chemical Company's earnings as follows:

"Earnings Reported	xxxxxxxxxxx
Add: Excess Depreciation after 50% tax	xxxxxxx
Earnings including excess depreciation	xxxxxxx

[2]Most analysts feel that the market tends to value oils, chemicals, and aluminum securities on a times cash earnings basis because of heavy depreciation charges.

and income taxes) divided by sales. Trends between years and between companies are examined in order that future expectations might be crystallized.

Jeremy Jenks has commented:

> Profit margins before taxes vary a good deal, particularly for the less well-integrated and less well-diversified companies. Perhaps the study of profit margins occupies more of security analysts' time than any other ratio and deservedly so, because, when an analyst can forecast an improvement in the profit margin, such as occurred in American Cyanamid between 1948 when the pretax margin was 7.6 per cent of sales and 1950 when it was 21.6 per cent of sales, or the even more startling example of Corning Glass, it is extremely rewarding to the investor.[1]

Analysts' reports invariably attempt to determine the primary causes for changing margins and also compare margins within industries. The following excerpt from an analysis of Marshall Field and Company is indicative of the analyst's approach:

> [First there appears an eight-year tabulation of operating profit margins of six department stores.]
> Though Field does not enjoy the highest operating profit margins in the industry, they are above average and have been, relatively, very stable. Analyzing 1948 and 1949 results, of the companies compared, Field and Federated did by far the best job of controlling the decline in margins. In the 1950-1951 period Field's margin declined less than any of the companies listed. On the other hand, Field was the only company which was unable to show a higher margin in 1952 than in 1951. Remodeling activities in the Frederick and Nelson Seattle store accounted, in part at least, for the poor profit margin showing for 1952. In general Federated and Field appear to have done the best job of controlling operating profit margins in the period since World War II.

Analysts naturally like seeing healthy pre-tax margins. They take a dim view of the future for companies whose margins are relatively low. The former viewpoint is best illustrated by an excerpt from an analysis of the Hazel-Atlas Glass Company. These excerpts follow in order:

---

[1]Jenks, <u>op. cit.</u>, p. 101.

[du Pont] Earlier in this Memorandum we showed the 18-year record of du Pont in relation to the composite results of Seven Major Chemical Companies. Three facts stand out from this comparative record: 1) du Pont has shown real growth during the period, particularly in pretax earnings; 2) its profit margin has been consistently and significantly higher than average; and 3) even at an all-time high price for du Pont Common (111), investors are paying no premium for du Pont's superior growth and position.

The table following views the record from a somewhat different angle and also shows the superior results of du Pont including the effectiveness of its postwar plant investment.

	Sales Per $1.00 Gross Plant		Indicated Profit Margin	
	du Pont[a]	Average of 7 Chem. Cos.[b]	du Pont[a]	Average of 7 Chem. Cos.[b]
1946	$1.11	$1.02	22.0%	16.8%
1947	1.23	1.22	21.0	17.8
1948	1.30	1.18	20.3	17.5
1949	1.23	1.07	23.9	19.2
1950	1.42	1.33	30.9	25.5
1951	1.50	1.44	32.6	25.0
1952	1.42	1.19	31.2	19.7
1953[c]	1.51	1.23	32.7	20.4

[a]Chemical operations only and excludes General Motors dividend.

[b]Allied Chemical, American Cyanamid, Dow, du Pont, Hercules Powder, Monsanto, and Union Carbide.

[c]Nine months ended September 30, 1953.

[Hazel-Atlas Glass] Hazel-Atlas is the second largest domestic producer of glass containers but with about 40 per cent of its sales accounted for by food containers it is not as broadly diversified as are some other glass container companies. Growth prospects for the industry are not imposing and Hazel-Atlas, with the major portion of its sales in products whose profit margins are relatively low and whose growth prospects are least impressive, is unlikely to match the growth of other industry leaders.

Income Taxes

The widespread practice of combining all income taxes into one figure is not welcomed by the analyst. When excess profits taxes were in force, the analyst was particularly interested in these amounts, both as to totals and on a per share basis. Jeremy Jenks has observed:

> About the only thing that can be said in favor of the EPT law is that it minimizes the impact of a substantial fluctuation in profit margins on net after taxes. For example, in 1951 Pfizer had pretax earnings of $40 million on $100 million of sales or a margin of 40 per cent. After a 70 per cent tax, profit was $12,250,000. This year on about the same sales, net before taxes may be on the order of $20 million, a margin of 20 per cent, half the level in 1951, but, after accruing taxes at the normal and surtax rate, earnings may be close to $10 million or only a little lower than a year ago.[1]

The analyst is interested in coupling material non-recurring items with income tax effects; he is also interested in income taxes on foreign operations. The former issue is discussed in detail in Chapter VI. If there are any substantial differences between reported income to stockholders and reported income for income tax purposes, the analyst desires a reconciliation of the two figures.[2] The Committee on Corporate Information formally recommended the following as a primary requirement for annual reports:

> The amount of income on which income tax was computed and an explanation of any significant differences between income for tax purposes and income as reported to stockholders. In addition, the amount of Federal income tax and Federal excess profit tax should be stated as separate items.[3]

Foreign Operations

Foreign operations contribute in substantial proportions to over-all sales in many industries.[4] The accounting practices

---

[1] Ibid.

[2] Benhamin Graham and D. Dodd, Security Analysis (3rd.; New York: McGraw-Hill Book Co., Inc., 1951), p. 173.

[3] Committee on Corporate Information, "Fourth Annual Report," op. cit., p. 216.

[4] Examples of industries having sizable foreign activities include motion pictures, office machines, chemicals, rubber, and mining.

with respect to consolidating foreign subsidiaries vary considerably; in general the state of disclosure concerning foreign operations is woefully inadequate.[1] Analysts feel that there is little reason why companies should not furnish at least the same essential data regarding foreign operations that is currently given concerning domestic operations. That is, firms should publish details such as sales, expenses, income taxes and total investments in foreign operations.

What format should be used in the presentation of such information? Analysts tend to favor consolidating all foreign subsidiaries on the same basis as consolidations of domestic

---

[1]Research Department, op. cit., p. 161, reports the following variety in current practice:

Foreign Subsidiaries

Basis of consolidation	1952	1951
Stated:		
All foreign subsidiaries consolidated	20	19
Wholly owned foreign subsidiaries consolidated. . . .	5	4
Based on stated percentage of ownership	6	4
Based on geographic location.	14	12
Based on geographical location and ownership.	4	4
All foreign subsidiaries excluded from consolidation.	22	21
	71	64
Indicated:		
By inclusion of all foreign subsidiaries in consolidation.	74	78
By exclusion of all foreign subsidiaries from consolidation.	59	61
	133	139
Not Determinable:		
Certain foreign subsidiaries consolidated	26	28
	230	231
Number of Companies Showing		
Foreign subsidiaries only	46	44
Both foreign and domestic subsidiaries.	184	187
Domestic subsidiaries only.	255	256
No subsidiary companies	115	113
	600	600

subsidiaries. In addition a detailed picture of the foreign operations themselves should be drawn either with separate formal statements or by means of footnotes.

An illustration of the basis of consolidation and presentation in financial statements which was welcomed by analysis is illustrated by the following excerpt from the 1953 annual report of the Burroughs Corporation:

> As in prior years, the statement of income includes the income and costs of all subsidiary companies. The net income of subsidiary companies operating outside the U.S. and Canada, less dividends paid to the parent company, has been deducted in arriving at "net" income for the year from operations in the U.S. and Canada, including dividends received from foreign operations.[1]

It is noteworthy that in the case of Burroughs, as in most other cases, the analyst is forced to contact sources other than the annual report to obtain a breakdown of sales and expenses between domestic and foreign operations.

Balance Sheet

The analysts' attitudes toward the balance sheet in nearly all cases is illustrated by the following excerpt from the report of the Subcommittee on Annual Reports of Drug Companies of the Committee on Corporate Information:

> Generally speaking, the balance sheet of an ethical drug company is not of great significance other than for showing the current position and the amount and location of the company's assets and capitalization. Because of the rapidly changing nature of the business the relationship of plant to sales and other ratios of this type are only of academic interest.[2]

---

[1] Burroughs Corporation, Annual Report, 1953.

[2] Subcommittee on Annual Reports of Drug Companies, *op. cit.*, p. 4.

Of primary interest to the analyst when balance sheets are inspected is the capitalization of the firm. Analysts' written reports almost always contained analyses of the capitalization (both at book and market values). Comparisons of changes in capitalization structures are made so that the financial policies of the corporation may be appraised.

By relating debt service requirements and dividend policies to the capitalization, the impact of possible future events upon the ability to meet obligations is determined. In addition, if any new financing will be needed, by comparing past financial policies and present financial position the analyst can estimate the type and amount of financing that probably will be undertaken. The following passages from an analysis of the Aluminum Company of America are indicative of the nature of the analyst's interest in capitalization structure:

> Alcoa's current financial position is no better than adequate and is not likely to improve greatly for some time because of planned heavy debt retirements. Cash declined about 26 per cent last year and equaled about one-fifth of current debt at the year end. Total current assets were less than one-half of total debt. Long-term debt of $295 million represented 41.3 per cent of the company's total capitalization, a rather high proportion for an industrial company but not unmanageable in this particular case because of the Government purchase contracts and the special tax provisions. . . .
>
> The company's current financial position is rather weak, reflecting the very heavy capital expenditures over the past few years but no further borrowing is indicated. The expansion program which has cost about $350 million is virtually completed and cash generated through amortization and depreciation will more than meet the heavy debt maturities through 1959. However, the continued need for cash will probably limit the dividend payout to the current $1.60 per share for some time.

There is no uniform pattern among analysts in dealing with balance sheet "reserves." When scanning a balance sheet, they decide whether such reserve credits are primarily retained earnings or liabilities in nature and classify them as such. For example, the reserves in Swift and Company's balance sheet are reported as restricted retained earnings.[1] Yet some analysts reclassified these reserves as liabilities.

As may be indicated by the Alcoa excerpt above, essentially "balance sheet analysis" is not concerned nearly so much with the financial position at a given instant of time as it is with the sources and applications of funds through the years. Thus "balance sheet analysis" is a misnomer; it really should be called a facet of "fund flow analysis."

Sources and Applications of Funds

Almost every analysis contains an estimate of sources and applications of funds over the past five to seven years and an estimate of fund flow for at least one year in advance. Analysts' written reports usually contain formal fund statements, but many written reports simply summarize the major sources and applications of funds in a paragraph or two.[2] Most annual reports of

---

[1]Swift and Co., Year Book, 1953.

[2]The following is an excerpt from an analysis of National Lead Company which is typical of the types of fund flow analyses drafted by analysts:

Flow of Funds: (Millions of Dollars)

	1951	1950
Net Income	$23.0	$26.5
Cash Dividends	16.5	15.6
Retained Earnings.	$ 6.5	$10.9
Per Cent Paid Out.	71.9%	58.8%
Depreciation	4.9	5.9
Net Cash Production.	$11.4	$16.8
Change in Stock.	..	+1.2
Total Available Cash	11.4	$18.0
Capital Expenditures	19.5	4.9
Other Changes, Net	- .6	- .6
Change in Working Capital.	$-7.5	$+12.5

companies do not contain funds statements. Therefore, in most cases the analyst uses balance sheets as the starting point in his fund analysis. A picture of the flow of funds is considered essential by the analyst because it offers the clearest quantitative insight into the financial policies of the firm and the future outlook for dividends. Consequently, it is evident from the <u>uses</u> of quantitative data by analysts that the funds statement ranks a close second to the income statement in utility, and that the balance sheet is a lagging third.[1]

The "fund flow" thinking of the analyst is exemplified by his treatment of fixed assets. The balance sheet values of fixed assets are all but ignored. Attention is concentrated upon capital expenditures over the past five to seven years, and, even more important, upon planned capital expenditures. The sources of the funds for capital expenditures and working capital requirements are also determined. By comparison of the sources and applications of funds the adequacy of the company financing is appraised. Extended treatment of this subject is found in Chapters VII and VIII. In general, analysts take a pessimistic view of the managements of companies who are not "keeping up with the Joneses of the industry."

The following excerpt from an investment analysis of the Dow Chemical Company is the skeleton of how the analyst projected the fund flow (specific figures are withheld) through 1957. It is significant that a projection was also made for the income

---

[1]Chapter VIII contains the writer's position that even the income statement is looked upon by the analyst as a detailed statement of funds provided by operations.

statement details but not for the balance sheet.

Projected Growth and Financing
(Through 1957)

Net Profit
Less Dividends Paid
  Retained Earnings
Depreciation
Accelerated Amortization
  Retained Cash Income
Premium on Sale of Stock
Premium on Conversion of Preferred
      TOTAL FUNDS PROVIDED
Plant Expenditures
 + (-) Working Capital
        TOTAL FUNDS APPLIED
Balance to be financed or
     (Available for repayment)
Increase in debt

Shares outstanding
Sales on rights
Stock dividends
Stock to employees

Per Share
Net Profit
Cash Dividends

If one considers the analysts' actions and needs, it seems obvious that one of the salient improvements in corporate annual reporting would be the inclusion of a flow of funds statement in every published report.

Summary

In summary, the following is a description of the financial analysts' approach to financial data:

1. They study financial statements from a comparative point of view. They look for trends and changes in major items. Comparisons between years, between products, and between similar firms are the uses which are made of the data. The primary reason for analyzing quantitative data is to secure clues as to

future performance. Figures are condensed. Anything under $100,000 (and sometimes $1 million) is generally regarded as insignificant.

2. The income statement is regarded as the most important reflector of the operations of the firm. There is a definite tendency to think in terms of "normal earning power," but all components of the statement are examined carefully. The leading items of interest include sales and sales breakdowns; cost of goods sold, inventory valuations, and gross margin; operating expenses such as research, long-term rentals, and depreciation; non-recurring items; foreign operations; income taxes; and net income. The most important ratio is considered to be net operating profit before income taxes divided by sales.

3. Analysts' concern with the balance sheet centers about an adequate current position and the structure of capitalization and any trends therein. Ratios most often employed are the current ratio and percentage breakdowns of capitalization structures. Reserves are scanned and reclassified where it is deemed necessary.

4. Much more important information than can be found in the balance sheet is gathered from a statement showing sources and applications of funds. Analysts either draft the latter statement or analyze comparative balance sheets in such a way that their written words amount to a funds flow analysis. Analysts are particularly interested in capital expenditures. They always try to relate outlays for plant and equipment to future sales and/or profits.

Why do analysts do what they do? The whys are not considered in this study because this investigation does not purport to present a crystallization of the interplay of the many factors that implement investment decisions. In perspective, if accounting can serve investors better, and still serve management, government and other interested parties just as well, then accounting is evolving in a desirable manner. Therefore, the uses of accounting information are the important factors, not why the uses are what they are. If the uses could or should change, then accounting must change as well. From the standpoint of this study the standard which must be applied in judging accounting is how well is it fulfilling its purpose of meeting the needs of professional investors. In turn, these needs flow from the uses of financial data by security analysts, whether or not these uses are considered to be sensible, canny, informed, or uninformed. For the most part analysts are very intelligent and sensible people. They know their business and they know what they need. It is doubtful that accountants and/or managers are justified in withholding or adjusting certain types of information sought by the analysts because the former feel that disclosure would be misleading or be subject to misinterpretation.

CHAPTER IV

INVENTORIES: ACCOUNTING PRACTICE

This and the following chapter will consider the financial analyst's problems concerning inventories. An attempt has been made to divide the discussion into two major divisions, (a) accounting practice and (b) the analyst's problems. However, there is some unavoidable overlapping--that is, some of the analyst's problems will be discussed in this chapter and some accounting practice will be presented in Chapter V.

This writer is indebted to Lester Greene, whose unpublished doctoral dissertation, "Financial Aspects of Inventory Valuation Methods,"New York University, 1953, greatly influenced my presentation in this and the following chapter.

Because the methods of inventory valuation have important implications in the measurement of reported income and in the analysis of current credit position, analysts are keenly interested in obtaining sufficient information about inventories. They desire (a) the segregation of inventories by classes; (b) the valuation bases used; (c) the replacement costs (or most recent costs) of the goods on hand; and (d) details of inventory reserve procedures.

Difficulties of Cost Determination

The choice of the specific method of inventory valuation has an important impact upon the measurement of income. Since "cost," determined in a multitude of ways, is the universal basis for the valuation of inventories, it must be emphasized that the cost of an inventory component is not the "actual," infallible measurement which many people feel it is. The estimation of "cost" as goods are purchased or manufactured is entwined in a web of difficulties. Each company utilizing "cost" as a basis for inventory valuations employs procedures developed by its own management. These procedures have grown in variety almost in direct proportion to the number of companies in existence.

The definition of cost as applied to incoming materials or merchandise is the first problem. What is "cost" in these cases? Is it part or all of the following: invoice price, freight charges, handling expenses, insurance, storage, purchasing department expenses, or any other indirectly or directly related charges?

Manufacturing operations are plagued by further difficulties. The most troublesome problems are the allocations of factory cost to units of product in cases of joint products and by-products, and to units of multiple products which pass through several departments. Complex formulae, "n" decimal places, simultaneous equations, and scrupulous reapportionments serve to cloud the reality that in essence the allocation of indirect costs is arbitrary. Preciseness is pretended where preciseness does not and cannot exist.

William J. Vatter has pointed to some implications for accountants in regard to cost allocations as follows:

> . . . the limitations of expediency, and the conflicting objectives that enter into cost calculations should make the

> accountant more careful as to his terminology with respect to unit costs. Readers of financial operating and cost reports, unless they are technically trained, are prone to accept terms used in accounting reports at their face value. The distinctly observable tendency toward emphasis of actuality in cost terminology is unfortunate . . . it is questionable whether there can be much hope of calculating an "actual" unit cost. . . . Cautious applications of terminology to figures that are subject to so many weaknesses, yet which can be taken to mean so much, are demanded by that prudence and judgment upon which the accountant's reputation depends.[1]

Once the cost procedures are settled upon, the question arises as to the method of allocation of product costs for the year between the goods sold and the goods on hand. Each of the many allocation methods yields a different result. There are many variations and combinations of first-in, first-out; last-in, first-out; a host of average cost methods; base stock, cost of specific units; standard costs; and retail methods. The mere grouping of methods gives some indication of the overwhelming task of cost allocation and, ultimately, income determination.

Current Accounting Methods

Undoubtedly the most exhaustive detailed survey of corporate reporting practices is found in the annual survey of 600 annual reports by the Research Department of the American Institute of Accountants. The results of the survey are printed annually in Accounting Trends and Techniques, a publication of the Institute.

What is current practice in inventory pricing? Trends and Techniques (1953 edition covering 1952 reports) states that of the 600 annual reports surveyed, only five did not disclose their inventory pricing basis. Four hundred and eighty-eight

---

[1]William J. Vatter, "Limitations of Overhead Allocation," Accounting Review, XX, No. 2 (April, 1945), 176.

"lower of cost or market" bases were reported, and 199 "cost" bases were reported. The bases reported exceeded the number of companies because many firms apply different bases of valuation to their holdings of various types of inventory.[1]

Although "market" is superimposed upon it in some cases, "cost" is still the fundamental method of valuation. But it is noteworthy that 222 out of 595 companies (nearly 40 per cent) reporting a cost basis failed to state their method of computing "cost." Of the 372 companies which revealed their method, 187 used lifo; 133, fifo; and 127, average cost. Again, methods reported exceeded the number of companies for the reason stated in the preceding paragraph.[2]

The failure of so many companies to reveal their cost methods is not as alarming as one might imagine. A sample check of companies not disclosing any method of determining cost garnered twenty-four replies out of forty inquiries. The following valuation methods were mentioned:

10 Fifo only
4 Fifo and average cost
4 Average cost only
2 Actual and average cost
2 Average cost, standard cost, and fifo
1 Lifo and average cost

Excerpts from letters received plus the predominance of fifo in the above tabulation would seem to indicate that some companies consider this method to be so well established or so generally accepted that its consistent use makes any reference to costing

---

[1] Research Department of the American Institute of Accountants, Accounting Trends and Techniques, 1953 edition (New York: American Institute of Accountants, 1953), p. 67.

[2] Ibid.

methods unnecessary in the annual report.[1]

The "cost" method of valuation sometimes is a modified cost basis. That is, the report indicates the inventories are at cost, but then further comments modify the method to cost or market. In its listing statement to the New York Stock Exchange, National Steel Corporation describes its inventory as being stated generally at cost on a life basis. Nevertheless adjustments are made, if required, to write items down to replacement market or selling market if lower than life cost.[2]

If one assumes that the vast majority of the 222 companies not stating their inventory cost method use predominantly fifo or average cost, then it is clear that the latter methods are still the most widely used. While use of lifo has become increasingly important, it still ranks below fifo and average cost.

After the first three methods the others are relatively unimportant. Standard cost, being mentioned 30 times, is generally limited to the machinery group and other capital goods industries.[3]

Last-In, First-Out

Adoption of Lifo

In the past fifteen years the last-in, first-out lifo method of determining cost has vaulted into prominence in

---

[1]Carman G. Blough (ed.), Current Accounting Problems, "Disclosure in Annual Reports of Methods of Determining Cost," Journal of Accountancy, LXXXVII, No. 2 (February, 1949), 157.

[2]National Steel Corporation, Listing statement to the New York Stock Exchange, March 27, 1950, p. 9.

[3]Research Department, op. cit., p. 67.

corporate accounting and finance. The years in which 176 manufacturing companies adopted lifo are as follows:

Table 1

ADOPTION OF LIFO

Year	Number of Companies
Before 1939	13
1939	11
1940	8
1941	62
1942	39
1943	8
1944	4
1945	3
1946	7
1947	21
	176

Source: J.K. Butters, Effects of Taxation: Inventory Accounting and Policies (Boston: Harvard University, 1949), p. 62.

In addition Trends and Techniques indicates that since 1947 at least five companies adopted lifo in 1948, forty-three in 1950, twenty-six in 1951, and three in 1952.[1] Since Butters' survey covers practically all publicly owned corporations, it would mean that at least 250 of them now use lifo.

The price rises and the excess-profits taxes accompanying the Korean outbreak were major factors in the rise in lifo bases from 115 in 1949 to 183 in 1951. Lifo companies in 1947 accounted for 19 per cent of the 600 companies tabulated, while in 1952 this percentage was up to 31 per cent.

The major shifts to lifo over the period 1949 to 1951

---

[1]Research Department, op. cit., p. 74.

were accounted for largely in the steel, rubber, machinery and paper industries. Of twenty-nine steel companies, five were using lifo in 1949 and sixteen in 1951. Rubber concerns on lifo increased from one to four, as Goodyear, Goodrich, and Firestone joined General Tire in the lifo ranks. Paper companies using lifo rose from four to nine. Of seventy-six machinery companies, lifo was only used by seven in 1949; by 1951 this number increased to eighteen.[1]

Lifo is most popular in the following industries:

Table 2

INDUSTRIAL CONCENTRATION OF LIFO--1952
(Based on sample of 600 Companies)

Industry	Group Total	No. of Firms Using Lifo
1. Nonferrous Metals.	18	14
2. Floor Covering	7	6
3. Steel and Iron	29	18
4. Agricultural Machinery . .	7	4
5. Petroleum.	32	18
6. Canning and Preserving . .	16	9
7. Wool and Cotton.	24	13
8. Meat Products.	12	6
9. Retail Stores.	36	12

Source: Research Department of the American Institute of Accountants, Accounting Trends and Techniques, 1953 ed. (New York: American Institute of Accountants, 1953), p. 75.

There are indications that the use of lifo is more concentrated in the larger companies. Butters has prepared, as of the end of 1947, figures on the relation of total inventories of lifo companies to total inventories of 548 companies on a lifo

[1]Research Department, op. cit., p. 75.

and non-lifo basis. A summary of his tabulation reveals the following:

Table 3

CONCENTRATION OF LIFO INVENTORIES
(in millions of dollars)

Assets	Companies		Total Inventories	Total Inventories Lifo Companies*	
	Total	Lifo	All Companies	Amount	Per Cent of Inventories All Companies
$0-under 10	187	26	$ 265	36	13.7
10-under 50	251	63	1,361	450	33.1
50-under 100	57	22	1,001	432	43.1
100-under 500	59	30	2,913	1626	55.8
500-and over	15	11	2,091	1524	72.9
	548	152	7,631	4068	53.3

*Aggregate valuation including other bases.

Source: Butters, Effects of Taxation, cited in Table 1, p. 60. Of 548 firms in the sample, 152 or 28 per cent using lifo in whole or part accounted for 53 per cent of the total inventories.

Application of Lifo

While a large number of corporations use lifo, there is little uniformity in the extent to which firms apply this method to their total inventory. In the textile field, for example, Bigelow-Sanford uses lifo only for material costs, while Cannon Mills is completely on a lifo basis. On the other hand, Burlington Mills applied lifo in 1947 to less than $1.0 million of a $32. million inventory. Another example is found in the meat-packing industry. Morrell and Rath value only pork products on a lifo basis, while Swift states that all but a small portion of its products is on lifo.[1]

[1]Carman G. Blough (ed.), Current Accounting Problems. "Use of Lifo by Industry Groups," Journal of Accountancy, LXXXVI, No. 1 (July, 1948), 69.

The following summary illustrates the wide variety of practice in applying lifo to total inventories:

Table 4

LIFO INVENTORY AS A PERCENTAGE OF TOTAL INVENTORIES FOR TWO INDUSTRIES: 1947

Textiles		Foods	
Company	Lifo Inventory as Per Cent of Total Inventory	Company	Lifo Inventory as Per Cent of Total Inventory
Pacific Mills	1.3	Clinton Indus.	11.3
Burlington Mills	2.0	Carnation	11.7
M. Lowenstein	4.9	Amer. Molasses	12.3
United Merchants	6.3	Seeman Bros.	17.1
J.P. Stevens	10.4	Kellogg	20.7
Textron	41.1	Wesson Oil and Snowdrift	50.7
Reeves	49.4	Libby, McNeill, and Libby	51.4
Kendall	74.7	California Pkg.	61.3
American Yarn	82.3	Holly Sugar	73.4
Wm. Whitman	90.7	Utah-Idaho Sugar	79.7
Archer-Daniels-Midland	8.7		

Source: Butters, cited in Table 1, pp. 282-83, 276-77.

The growth of the use of lifo has added to the woes of the analyst in many ways. The major problems which have arisen will be discussed in the next chapter.

Inventory Reserves

Variety of Inventory Reserves

The approaches of corporations with respect to inventory reserves demonstrate how varied and confusing inventory accounting can be. Inventory reserves can be segregated into two primary classifications, (a) valuation reserves, which directly reduce inventories and hence affect income determination, and (b) retained earnings reserves, which are signals to the reader that management fears possible <u>future</u> inventory price declines. Thus inventory reserves must be dissected in terms of their various purposes.

The following table indicates current practice with regard to inventory reserves:

Table 5

INVENTORY RESERVES

Number of Companies	1952	1951	1950	1949
Setting forth inventory reserves . . .	108	114	123	131
Not setting forth inventory reserves. .	492	486	477	469
	600	600	600	600
Purpose Stated				
Possible future inventory price decline	36	42	50	68
Obsolescence in inventory	18	18	19	17
Basic life inventory replacement. . .	14	15	15	9
Reduction to cost basis	11	11	12	10
Reduction to market	3	1	1	1
Miscellaneous purposes.	21	22	23	23
Purpose not stated.	23	23	25	29
	127	132	145	157

Source: Research Department, cited in Table 2, p. 78

The balance sheet presentations of these reserves reflect widely varying practices. Reserves were classified most often in the current asset section with the related inventories (49 reserves). Thirty-five reserves were found above the stockholders' equity section, and twenty-six reserves were within that section.[1]

Inventory reserves which supplement fifo or average cost have been used for many years. Before the general use of lifo,

[1]Research Department, <u>op. cit</u>., p. 79.

firms wishing to exclude inventory "profits" or "losses" from income used an inventory reserve or the base stock method. Inventory reserves were more widely used, however, than base stock. American Woolen, for example, as far back as 1917 established a substantial reserve for possible shrinkage of war-inflated inventories. The company used this reserve to absorb heavy losses following World War I.[1]

The problem of valuation reserves versus retained earnings reserves is further complicated by the determination of the proper <u>amounts</u> which are to be charged or credited to reserves each year. As can be seen from the examples which follow, objective criteria are often not applied. Thus the amounts are arbitrary in many instances. In other cases objective criteria are used and a fairly consistent policy is maintained from year to year.

Discretionary Reserves

The following are three examples of the type of reserve which has been subjected to considerable criticism. Discretionary reserves, which are manipulated without objective standards and without an adequate way to check the judgment of those determining the amounts, should be eliminated.

From 1946 to 1948 American Woolen built up a reserve for contingencies for possible inventory declines aggregating $8.0 million. In 1949 $2.1 million of this reserve was transferred to earned surplus to offset an inventory writedown of the same

---

[1]C.W. Gerstenberg, Financial Organization and Management of Business, 2nd rev. ed. (New York: Prentice-Hall, Inc., 1939), p. 583.

amount. The unused balance of the reserve was carried as part of earned surplus.[1]

In 1947 Westinghouse charged income in order to create a reserve for future inventory losses of $8.1 million. This reserve was established because of the hazard existing in the high price level. The provision was based on "the opinion of management." Westinghouse's auditors commented on the company's discretionary reserve in their certificate.[2]

Although the Borden Company uses lifo for part of its inventory, in 1946 it nevertheless established a reserve of $5 million from surplus for possible inventory price declines. The firm pointed out that it "was aware of the disastrous drop in commodity prices during the period following World War I but anticipated no similar decline in 1947."[3]

Reserves Applying Criteria

A second type of reserve is more defensible in a sense because it is based on some standard of measurement. Proctor and Gamble and Pacific Mills illustrate this type of reserve.

Proctor and Gamble, before its adoption of lifo, used a reserve for protection against decline in inventory prices. As can be seen in the table which follows, in the postwar period this reserve stabilized reported earnings during the inflationary years of 1947 and 1948 and during the deflationary year of 1949.

---

[1]American Woolen Company, Annual Reports, 1947-1949.

[2]J.K. Butters, Effects of Taxation: Inventory Accounting and Policies (Boston: Harvard University, 1949), p. 252.

[3]Borden Company, Annual Report, 1946, p. 14.

Table 6

PROCTOR AND GAMBLE COMPANY
NET INCOME, 1947-1950

Year Ended June 30	Net Income Before Inventory Reserve*	Change in Reverse for Inventory Price Decline	Net Income
1947	$46,924	$14,000	$32,924
1948	65,419	23,000	42,419
1949	28,655	(21,000)	49,655
1950	61,092	0	61,092

*In thousands of dollars

Source: Proctor and Gamble Company, Annual Reports, 1947-1950.

A financial executive of Pacific Mills described his firm's system as follows: "Watching with alarm increasing raw material prices, the company, which is not on lifo, started a reserve for contingencies in 1941 and has added to it as raw material prices have risen. This reserve approximates the amount of profit which was necessary to invest in future raw material inventories at higher costs and is an approximation of the overstatement of published profits due to the inventory appreciation."[1] He also stated that in case of loss Pacific Mills will charge the loss to the reserve. But if the reserve is not needed it will be credited to surplus.[2]

Reserves to Secure Life-Equivalent

Another type of reserve which merits scrutiny is the reserve to secure a lifo-equivalent valuation. In 1952 only six

[1]Profits. Report of a Subcommittee of the Joint Committee on the Economic Report on Profit Hearings (Washington, D.C.: U.S. Government Printing Office, 1949), p. 338.

[2]Ibid., p. 339.

out of the 600 company sample used this type of reserve.[1] Pittsburgh Plate Glass Company offers an example of this procedure. In 1946 the firm established a $4.0 million reserve for market declines. It was estimated at that time that this reserve would approximate the effect of valuing inventories of certain commodities on a lifo basis. However, in 1947 the company decided to make an actual statement of inventory of flax, linseed oil, and bristle on a lifo basis. "The reserve deducted at December 31, 1947 represents the amount necessary to reduce to a last-in, first-out basis inventories of these commodities valued at $8,238,569 on an average cost basis."[2]

Pittsburgh Plate Glass has followed a consistent policy of adjusting cost of sales for estimated inventory profits and losses on certain commodities. The postwar picture shown below demonstrates the profit-dampening influence of this reserve:

Table 7

PITTSBURGH PLATE GLASS COMPANY, NET INCOME, 1946-1949

Year	Net Income Before Reserve Revisions*	Provision for Reserve to Secure Lifo Equivalent	Net Income
1946	$21.0	$-4.0	$17.0
1947	32.6	-4.9	27.7
1948	37.4	-4.7	32.7
1949	40.4	-2.3	38.1

*In millions of dollars

Source: Pittsburgh Plate Glass Co., Annual Reports, 1946-1949.

[1]Research Department, *op. cit.*, p. 75.

[2]Pittsburgh Plate Glass Co., *Annual Report, 1947*, p. 18.

The reserve to secure a lifo equivalent is not recognized for tax purposes. Thus the tax effects usually will be shown as computed under fifo application. Therefore reported income will often differ substantially from taxable income.

Colgate-Palmolive Peet exemplifies the attempt by firms to adjust for inventory "profits" and "losses" in the income statement. This company described its reserve for inventory price decline as a "segregation of earnings made to give the company protection in its accounts against losses arising from a drop in the market price of raw materials."[1] Later comment included, "when a decline in the price level occurs, inventories previously purchased at high prices may have to be sold below their cost. We are keenly aware of this situation and try to take precautions to minimize such losses."[2]

The following summary portrays the influence of the reserve upon earnings:

Table 8

COLGATE PALMOLIVE PEET CO., NET INCOME, 1946-1949

Year	Net Income Before Changes in Inventory Reserve*	Changes in Inventory Reserve	Net Income
1946	$17,944	$+3500	$14,444
1947	22,764	+3750	19,014
1948	7,557	-4250	11,807
1949	11,076	-3000	14,076

*In thousands of dollars

Source: Colgate-Palmolive Peet Co., Annual Reports 1946-1949

[1] Colgate-Palmolive Peet Co., Annual Report, 1948, p. 7.

[2] Ibid., 1949, p. 9.

In 1946 and 1947 a total of $7.3 million was segregated as representing the company's estimate of future losses. In 1948, $4.3 million was credited to surplus to allow for inventory losses, and in 1949 the balance of $3.0 million was transferred to surplus as partial compensation for inventory declines. Actually, the losses in 1948 and 1949 were greater than the balance in the reserve.

General-Purpose Reserves

The final type of reserve which needs scrutiny is the "general-purpose catch-all" which is illustrated by the examples which follow.

From 1941 to 1947 General Foods Corporation set aside $10.0 million as additions to its reserve for contingencies for possible inventory losses and "other unpredictable contingencies." The company stated: "In view of the continued high level of commodity prices during 1948, the Board made an addition of $1,500,000 to this reserve. The Reserve for Contingencies represents an appropriation of earnings retained in the business but will not be used to relieve future income of charges properly applicable thereto.[1] In another instance the firm mentioned that its contingency reserve set up out of surplus "serves as a warning to stockholders and investors to the potential danger in our inventories due to very high raw material prices."[2]

Food Machinery Corporation emphasized the mixed nature of its reserve for contingencies when it described it as follows:

---

[1] General Foods Corporation, Annual Report, 1948, p. 15.

[2] Profits, p. 47.

"This reserve has been accumulated from earnings in past years as a protection to our stockholders against inventory losses, obsolesence of leased machinery, and other unforeseen contingencies."[1]

Pacific Mills, in recognition of the general purpose buffer nature of its inventory reserve, transferred it to earned surplus and explained: "The same purpose is served by including this amount in Earned Surplus of which it really is a part."[2]

In 1947 Link Belt Company closed its inventory reserve to earned surplus after concluding "that nothing is to be gained by deducting any specific amount from our substantial surplus and designating it as a reserve."[3]

As can be seen from the above examples there are conflicting opinions as to the desirability of earmarking retained earnings for such purposes as possible future price declines. Opposing views probably will never be reconciled. Meanwhile, the analyst must sift through company after company and become thoroughly acquainted with widely varying practices.

Decreasing Importance of Reserves

Inventory reserves charged against income have decreased from 21 per cent of the sample companies in 1947 to 13 per cent in 1949 to 8 per cent in 1952. Appropriations of retained earnings have also declined. There are three major reasons for the decreases.

---

[1]Food Machinery Corporation, Annual Report, 1950, p. 10.

[2]Pacific Mills Inc., Annual Report, 1949, p. 11.

[3]Link Belt Company, Annual Report, 1947, p. 9.

First, widespread adoption of lifo has reduced the necessity for reserves. Proctor and Gamble, a long-time user of the reserve method, stated that adoption of lifo in 1950 minimizes the effects of inventory profits and losses and the "need no longer exists for the reserve for inventory price decline."[1]

Second, the American Institute of Accountants and the Securities and Exchange Commission have frowned upon the inclusion of reserve adjustments in the computation of net income.[2] For example, in 1948 Mohawk Carpet Mills returned $1.5 million in the inventory reserve to earned surplus because the S.E.C. would not allow losses to be charged to the reserve.[3]

Third, in some instances anticipated price declines have never materialized. In 1951 Pillsbury Mills discontinued its reserve for inventory valuation. This reserve was established to reduce unhedged commodities to 1946 price levels. The expectation that prices would recede to 1946 levels was not borne out, and the management concluded that prices would not fall below 1950 levels in the foreseeable future.[4]

Summary of Accounting Practice

The important points concerning current accounting practice with respect to inventories may be summarized as follows:

1. Cost or market is still the most prevalent valuation rule. Use of cost alone has increased in recent years because

---

[1] Wall Street Journal (August 13, 1951), p. 5.

[2] Committee on Accounting Procedure, American Institute of Accountants, Accounting Research Bulletin No. 43: Restatement and Revision of Accounting Research Bulletins (New York: The American Institute of Accounts, 1953), p. 41.

[3] Mohawk Carpet Mills, Annual Report, 1948, p. 12.

[4] Pillsbury Mills, Inc., Annual Report, 1951.

of the rise of lifo.

2. The most common costing techniques are still fifo and average cost, which are about equally popular. In the Institute survey in 1952 only five companies out of 600 used base stock. Cost methods other than average cost, fifo, and lifo are relatively insignificant.

3. The great rise in lifo over the past fifteen years is the outstanding feature of inventory valuation practice. The following are the primary observations about this relatively new valuation method:

(a) Lifo is the third most important valuation method.

(b) Lifo is used in many industries but is more heavily concentrated in those industrial groups most commonly plagued by inventory "profits" and "losses."

(c) The use of lifo is proportionately greater in larger companies.

(d) The quantities of inventories on lifo vary considerably among individual firms.

(e) The application of lifo is on a highly selective basis.

4. The handling of inventory reserves is probably the most confusing area of inventory accounting. Inventory reserves for possible future price declines, the most common type of reserve, has shown a steady decline in usage since 1947. This decline is attributable to the wider adoption of lifo, to pressure from the Institute and the S.E.C., and to the failure of price declines to materialize.

CHAPTER V

INVENTORIES: THE ANALYST'S PROBLEMS

Visualize the analyst who is confronted with the variegated pattern of accounting practice. He is concerned about the inventory situation because of the difficulties in making comparisons, especially between lifo and fifo companies and between lifo companies using different base years. The discriminating analyst attempts to obtain a meaningful comparison of companies within industries by developing, as far as practicable, a uniform inventory basis.

Is it adequate disclosure to reveal an inventory valuation method as "lower of cost or market," lifo, or average cost? Management seems to think so, as is evident by the state of reporting. Their reasons for not revealing more details generally revolve about the complexity of operations of the company, the burdensome and exhaustive explanations which would be required, and the doubts as to the importance of further disclosure.

The latter reason is buttressed by the stand that consistency in the employment of a specific method from year to year and a full indication in the financial statements of any alteration of method from year to year may yield sufficient protection to the analyst. But the analyst's needs and uses must not be neglected. His task is comparison. He is interested in a method of inventory valuation which reflects most clearly the income for a particular year or a short span of years. In addition, he desires more uniformity of inventory methods from firms within the same industry. And, most important currently, he needs more detailed information concerning inventory valuation methods so that he may obtain a useful basis of comparison of similar companies.[1]

It should be emphasized that except in extremely detailed analyses (i.e., in the case of underwriting a new issue of securities) the analyst does not formally adjust income results in order to place two or more companies on a comparable basis. Instead, he usually points out in his report that one company uses lifo and another uses fifo. Thus the analyst assumes that the reader will interpret the results as he sees fit. The most common reason for failing to alter results formally is that there is not sufficient information available to justify any meaningful adjustments.

In detailed analyses one of the fundamental problems facing the analyst is the recasting of lifo and fifo figures on a comparable basis. For purposes of comparison a substantially corresponding method of inventory valuation is applied to each company. Currently, in most cases the inventories and earnings of lifo firms are increased to conform with the conventional fifo method. Some companies on a lifo basis furnish the replacement figure for their inventory.[2] One of the most common complaints

---

[1]Committee on Corporate Information, "Fourth Annual Report," The Analysts Journal, VIII, No. 4 (August, 1952), 216, formally suggests disclosure of the following: "The FIFO value of LIFO inventory, and the per cent of total inventory carried on a LIFO basis."

[2]Holly Sugar Corporation is exemplary in this regard. Other

of the analysts interviewed was that not enough firms disclose this information.

The following example demonstrates the analyst's approach in his attempts to compare lifo and fifo companies within the same industry:

Calculation of Earnings of Federated and National Department Stores for the Year Ended January 1948 on a 100 Per Cent Lifo and 100 Per Cent Fifo Basis[1]

1. Reported Earnings. Federated reported earnings of $4.18 per share on lifo basis applied to 78 per cent of its inventory. National reported earnings of $4.12 per share on a fifo basis.

2. Calculation of the Per Cent of Devaluation of Discount Produced by Lifo. In January 1948, $21.8 million of Federated's inventory was carried on a lifo basis; it had a fifo value of $30.6 million. Hence the lifo price level was 71.5 per cent of the fifo level. Corresponding figures for January 1947 were not given. However, the annual report stated that the comparative price level had advanced 10.3 per cent in the year. Working back, we can calculate the lifo level in January 31, 1947, was 110.3 per cent of 71.5 per cent or 78.7 per cent of the fifo level.

3. Earnings on an All-Fifo Basis. These were supplied by both companies. For National they were $3,224,000, or $4.12 per share. For Federated they were $11,848,000, equivalent to $4.80 per share of common.

4. Earnings on an All-Lifo Basis. Neither company published this figure, but it can be estimated for both. Federated reported earnings on the lifo basis as applied to 78 per cent of its total inventory. If the devaluation factor calculated above had been applied to 100 per cent of the inventory, there would have been an additional markdown in 1948 of about $500,000 before taxes, or $300,000 after taxes. This would have reduced the reported earnings by 13 cents per share, an unimportant adjustment.

If National's inventories on the beginning and closing dates are converted to a lifo basis by use of the Federated devaluation factors, the January 1947 figure would be reduced from

---

firms which disclose replacement costs for lifo inventories include Allied Stores Corporation, The Borden Company, and the Caterpillar Tractor Company.

[1]B. Graham and D. Dodd, Security Analysis (3rd ed.; New York: McGraw-Hill Book Co., 1951), p. 688.

$11,124,000 to $8,750,000 and the January 1948 figure would be reduced from $12,037,000 to $8,600,000. Thus, the inventory would have declined $150,000 on a lifo basis instead of increasing $913,000 as it did on a fifo basis--a difference of $1,063,000. The net additional devaluation for the next year, after taxes, would be $640,000 or 81 cents per share--reducing the earnings, on a lifo basis, to $3.31.

5. Summary on a per-share basis.

	As Reported	Adjusted to 100 Per Cent Lifo	Adjusted to 100 Per Cent Fifo
Federated. . . .	$4.18	$4.05	$4.80
National	4.12	3.31	4.12

The Lifo Problems

Lifo, base stock and their various offshoots demand the exacting attention of the capable analyst. The growth of the adoption of lifo had generated several problems, not the least of which is the hampering of comparability of similar enterprises.[1] One lifo difficulty for analysts arises when there are temporary withdrawals of inventory below the normal physical quantities, thus releasing "old" costs to be matched against current revenues. Another lifo problem which challenges the analyst is the fall in replacement prices below lifo carrying values. Still another difficulty occurs because layers of inventory are added at various price levels when there are increases in the normal quantity of inventory over the years. Base stock and inventory reserve methods are often so shrouded in mystery that the analysts throw up their hands in despair and do not attempt adjustments.

[1]E.B. Wilcos, "The Rise and Fall of Lifo," Journal of Accountancy, LXXXV, No. 2 (February 1948), 100, made a pertinent observation in this regard: "[considering] . . . the growing demand for understandable uniformity in accounting procedure. Lifo is not helping to meet this challenge."

Liquidation of Lifo Stock

Let us consider the case of liquidation of part of the basic lifo stock. In such instances the lifo purpose of matching current costs with current revenues is defeated and reported profits veer upward because "old" costs are matched against current revenues. Three illustrations of this effect follow.

Bigelow-Sanford reported in 1949 that inventories which were higher than normal at the beginning of the year were reduced by the end of the year to a level more nearly normal to sales. The effect of this reduction in inventories was to release low cost wools and consequently create a "windfall" profit of $800,000 after taxes.[1]

In 1948 Cannon Mills sharply increased its earnings. But a large part of this gain was because "a substantial portion of the cotton inventories maintained on the lifo basis was liquidated, and since the valuation of such inventories was considerably lower than current replacement costs, the net income for the year is materially higher than it would have been had sales been wholly from current purchases of cotton at prevailing 1948 price levels." Cannon Mills did not report the profit attributable to selling out part of the base stock, but net income for 1948 was $26.1 million as against $15.1 million in 1947. The net income as a per cent of sales rose to 17.0 per cent in 1948 compared to 9.5 per cent in 1947.[2]

Wesson Oil and Snowdrift reported for the year ended August 31, 1948, that "substantial quantities of vegetable oils

---

[1]Bigelow-Sanford Company, Annual Report, 1949, pp. 12-13.

[2]Cannon Mills, Inc., Annual Report, 1948, p. 8.

carried in the accounts on a lifo basis were voluntarily liquidated resulting in a gross profit (before income taxes and other expenses) of approximately $12,000,000 largely because of the low carrying value of the oils sold."[1]

Voluntary reduction of quantities within the basic lifo inventories tends to create "unusual" profits which could be misleading when one considers the major purpose of lifo (matching current costs with current revenues). Although these profits are realized in the form of cash, their transitory nature should require management to distinguish them and to explain the circumstances as fully as possible.

Lifo Layers

There may be times when a lifo company will expand its lifo base with succeeding layers of higher cost goods. Should the price level turn downward sharply, the concern may suddenly find part of its lifo inventory valued above replacement cost. If the firm is following the cost or market rule in its financial statements, it will be necessary to write down that part of its lifo stock which it carried at a value above market.

American Smelting and Refining Company faced this problem in 1949 because of the marked drop in metal prices. The company pointed out that the price of lead was 21 1/2 cents a pound at the start of the year and was 12 cents at the end, a net decline of 44 per cent. The price of zinc also fell 44 per cent from 17 1/2 cents to 9 1/4 cents. Copper prices fell 21 per cent during the year. Consequently, as it was impossible to

[1]Wesson Oil and Snowdrift Company, Annual Report, 1948, p. 6.

liquidate large tonnages of non-ferrous metals accumulated earlier in 1949 at prices considerably higher than those prevailing at December 31, 1949, the company charged approximately $6.0 million to earnings. This write-down represented the difference between the cost of all metals and their market value at year-end.[1]

Lifo "Cushion"

The difference between lifo cost and replacement cost is often considered to be a "cushion" or reserve to absorb possible future price declines.[2] In 1949 Morrell and Company pointed out that the "bulk of our product inventories continues to be carried at the relatively low prices of November 2, 1940. There is a considerable difference between the current market value of the inventories and the value at which they are carried, and this constitutes a substantial reserve against future declines in product prices."[3]

Even though Caterpillar adopted lifo in the relatively high price period at January 1, 1949, it still had a substantial "cushion." "At the end of 1949, the replacement cost of the company's inventories was approximately $64,200,000 as compared with the amount of $54,016,134 reported in the financial statements, an excess of 19 per cent. Cost levels can therefore decrease proportionately before the amounts of inventories and

---

[1]American Smelting and Refining Company, Annual Report, 1949, p. 7.

[2]For an extended discussion of the ramifications of the lifo "cushion" see Carman G. Blough, "LIFO Inventory Accounting in a Period of Declining Prices," The Analysts Journal, V, No. 2 (May, 1949), 12-14.

[3]John Morrell and Company, Annual Report, 1949, p. 11.

profits would have to be written down."[1]

Bigelow-Sanford stated, "The market value of the materials contained in our inventory at December 31, 1948 was approximately $10,000,000 above the figure at which they were carried on our balance sheet."[2]

R.H. Macy and Company reported, "At July 31, 1948, the cumulative reduction in the inventory valuation by the use of the lifo method amounted to $12,719,314, equal to approximately 34 per cent of the inventories valued at present price levels, thus providing a substantial cushion against shrinkage in future earnings resulting from price decline."[3]

Financial analysts have considerable interest in the lifo "cushion" and have expressed a desire to know its amount. They want to know the probable effects upon a company's financial reporting if the price level begins to go down. Is the cushion likely to be significant if there is a marked fall in the market? The amount of the cushion depends upon the following factors: (a) the proportion of the total inventories on lifo; (b) the time in the price cycle when lifo was adopted; and (c) the layers of lifo inventory carrying different prices. Without this kind of information the analyst is forced to speculate about the amount of the cushion. Considering the pitfalls of such a speculation it is understandable that the analyst feels that such information should be forthcoming from the companies themselves.

---

[1]Caterpillar Tractor Company, Annual Report, 1949, p. 23.

[2]Bigelow-Sanford Company, Annual Report, 1948, p. 10.

[3]R.H. Macy and Company, Annual Report, 1948, p. 12.

Inventory Profits

Many analysts feel that one of the major shortcomings of financial reporting is the widespread failure of concerns to disclose information about physical units of production and/or inventories.[1] Obviously such information is most significant in industries where "inventory profits" (and losses) are material items. Inventory profits are additional profits arising from the sale in a rising market of lower cost inventory carried forward from an earlier accounting period. These additional profits are reflected in the higher-cost units which are included in year-end inventory as replacements for those goods sold.

Ways of estimating inventory profits include the following:

(a) Difference between net income as computed by lifo and fifo

(b) Annual appropriation for a reserve for inventory declines, where it is meant to approximate the price rise in unit inventory values.

(c) The annual charge to provide for a reserve that brings fifo inventories down to a "lifo equivalent."

In appraising the use of lifo by a firm it is important to obtain the percentage of total inventory on lifo and the vulnerability of the non-lifo items to price changes. Even reported profits for companies using lifo may include an element of inventory profit attributable to the non-lifo segments of the inventory,

---

[1]A stimulating discussion of inventory profits will be found in Arundel Cotter, <u>Fool's Profits</u> (New York: Barron's Publishing Co., 1940), pp. 47-51, pp. 92-101, 149-151.

since very few lifo firms use the basis for the entire inventory.[1]

The following examples demonstrate the type of information which the analyst welcomes as being better than average reporting in this area.

Swift and Company adopted lifo as of October 1, 1940. The effect on the year ended November 1, 1941 was to decrease reported income approximately $7.0 million after taxes. This $7.0 million, representing inventory profit, if added to the $17.8 million reported under the lifo basis, would have increased net income to $24.8 million had the old method been continued.[2] For the fiscal year ending in 1942, inventory profits were $2.2 million before taxes but only $400,000 after taxes.[3] After 1942 Swift discontinued making the comparison under the two methods.

American Viscose adopted lifo in 1947 and showed the differences under lifo and fifo for 1947 and for 1948. The result was that net profit for 1947 was reported as $18.5 million after the elimination of $2.1 million of inventory profits. Net profits in 1947 would have been 11.4 per cent higher if fifo had been continued.[4] In 1948 this firm reported net income of $29.1

---

[1]Graham and Dodd point out how misleading comparisons can be made between two lifo companies by demonstrating the divergent results of Swift and Company and Armour and Company between 1945 and 1949. Both firms stated that they were on a lifo basis as to part of their inventory, but they did not supply data as to the dollar amounts involved in that portion and in the other. B. Graham and D. Dodd, op. cit., p. 118.

[2]Swift and Company, Yearbook, 1941, p. 8.

[3]Ibid., Yearbook 1942, p. 9.

[4]American Viscose Corporation, Annual Report, 1947, p. 15.

million under lifo, and $30.7 million if fifo had been used.[1]

Holly Sugar Corporation's financial reporting is especially commendable in that the firm shows the net income under fifo and lifo since it adopted lifo in 1942. The reports indicate some interesting differences even during World War II. A comparison is given below of net income after taxes. Also included for comparison is the inventory "cushion," which represents the amount by which lifo is lower than fifo, if the latter had been continued.

Inventory Profit of Holly Sugar Corporation
(Thousands of Dollars)

Fiscal Year Ending March 31	Net Income After Taxes		Inventory Profit		
	Fifo	Lifo	Amount	As a Per Cent of Fifo Net Income	Inventory Cushion*
1943	$1.140	$ .657	$ .483	42.4	$1.086
1944	1.040	-.574	1.614	155.2	1.600
1945	.600	.216	.384	64.0	.800
1946	.910	.680	.230	25.3	1.650
1947	1.930	.508	1.422	73.7	4.100
1948	3.030	2.166	.864	28.5	7.900

*Represents amount by which lifo inventory is lower than fifo at the end of years given.

Source: Holly Sugar Corporation, Annual Reports, 1943-1948.

Holly provides a good example of the influences of inventory "losses" upon reported income. For the year ending March 31, 1949, Holly reported that inventory losses were $750,000, and if fifo had been used, the net income would have been $744,000 after taxes. Since lifo showed a net income of $1,494,000, the effect

[1] _Ibid._, _Annual Report, 1948_, p. 13.

of avoiding the inclusion of inventory losses was to double the profit. For 1950, inventory losses increased to $1.2 million. The lifo method showed net income after taxes at $1.8 million as against $0.6 million if fifo had been continued. Certainly, inclusion of inventory profits and losses in the case of Holly Sugar would have materially changed the entire reported earnings picture.

National Supply Company affords the rare instance where a company actually states its estimated inventory profit in a dollar amount. The 1948 annual report of this company points out that its large increase in earnings for 1948 is misleading "Of the net earnings reported for 1948, probably $2,000,000 is represented by inventory profit due to price increases."[1] This was equal to about 16.0 per cent of the reported net income of $12.2 million. The percentage is high when one considers that the firm is partially on a lifo basis.

Dwight Billings, a financial officer of Pacific Mills, testified before a joint committee of Congress holding hearings on corporate profits that the inventory reserves used by his company approximate Pacific Mill's inventory profits.[2]

As final illustrations of inventory profits there are the firms which use inventory reserves to secure a lifo-equivalent. Sherwin-Williams Company deducted a reserve from certain raw materials to put them on a lifo basis, related to 1945 prices. The annual adjustment for this reserve is deducted before arriving at

---

[1]National Supply Company, Annual Report, 1948, p. 14.

[2]Profits. Report of a Subcommittee of the Joint Committee on the Economic Report on Profit Hearings (Washington, D.C.: U.S. Government Printing Office, 1949), p. 338.

net income. The amounts shown for 1947 and 1948 are $2.0 and $1.5 million respectively.[1]

Hercules Motors Corporation deducted $1.4 million prior to 1947, $849,000 in 1947, and $290,000 in 1948 and included these amounts as charges to Cost of Goods Sold in order to remove from income the inventory profit element. As a result, in 1948 inventory of $7.9 million was shown on a fifo basis with a reserve of $2.5 million deducted to give an inventory valuation at approximate 1942 price levels. Furthermore, in 1949 the firm offset its inventory loss of $410,000 by crediting that amount to Cost of Goods Sol

Differentiating between Price and Quantities

The following are a few examples of how some companies attempt to describe the quantity and price influences upon their respective inventory positions. Analysts desire more amplification in this area from all industrial corporations.[3]

Cudahy Packing offered the following analysis for 1947: "Our inventory at the close of the year amounted to $47,612,000, as compared with the total of $33,781,000 last year. Approximately $8,200,000 of this increase, or 60 per cent is due to an

---

[1]Sherwin-Williams Company, Annual Report, 1947, p. 9; 1948 p. 11.

[2]Hercules Motors Corporation, Annual Report, 1947, p. 18; 1948, p. 16; 1949, p. 16.

[3]Subcommittee on the Adequacy of Annual Reports of the Pap Industry, Committee on Corporate Information, The Analysts Journal VII, No. 2 (May, 1951), 146. Among the deficiencies with respect paper company annual reporting was the failure to disclose tonnage production of the major pulp and paper classifications. "Likewise, a record of the selling prices of the principal products should be included, so as to enable the analyst to determine to what extent any improvement in the company's business was due to higher prices or volume, or the reverse, if a company's sales were declining."

increase in products on hand, and the remaining 40 per cent to the higher cost of raw materials, labor and supplies."[1]

In 1948 Cudahy mentioned that, of its rise in inventories of $3,327,000, "$313,000 or 10 per cent of this increase results from an increase in products on hand and the remaining 90 per cent to higher price levels."[2]

Swift and Company mentioned in 1948 that its "prewar inventory of product . . . in other words the amount that we needed to fill our pipe lines of distribution stood at about 75 million dollars. With approximately the same tonnage of product in our pipe lines at the end of the 1947 fiscal year, our inventory represented a value of about 146 million dollars. In other words, operation at the year's end required the use of some 70 million dollars more than in 1939."[3]

Eagle Picher made the following comments: "The 1944 year-end metal inventory represented approximately the same tonnage as that at November 30, 1948, yet the value of the current inventory was some $7.0 million in excess of that of the earlier date."[4]

In 1947 Proctor and Gamble pointed out, "We actually have fewer pounds of raw materials in our inventory than we did in 1938, yet our dollar requirements for this purpose is more than double what it was at that time."[5]

---

[1]Cudahy Packing Company, Annual Report, 1947, p. 4.

[2]Ibid., 1948, p. 5.

[3]Roy Foulke, A Study of the Theory of Corporate Net Profits (New York: Dun and Bradstreet, 1949), p. 49.

[4]Eagle Picher Lead Company, Annual Report, 1948, p. 3.

[5]Foulke, op. cit., p. 50.

A final example is the case of Colgate in 1947, "As compared with the beginning of the year, inventories have increased $7,537,231, but quantities in relation to anticipated needs are generally lower."[1]

Problems of Inventory Reserves

Analysts would certainly agree with Butters' observations on inventory reserves: "Traditionally, inventory reserves have been established by such arbitrary criteria and have been handled in so many different ways . . . that their use has tended to confuse rather than clarify the statement of business income."[2]

As previous examples probably have indicated, the analyst needs detailed descriptions of inventory reserve procedures in order to deal intelligently with his problems of comparison. Probably the best manner of demonstrating what analysts do in regard to inventory reserves is to present passages from their written analyses in selected cases.

Marshall Field

Marshall Field has an example of a lifo-equivalent reserve. Notice in the following excerpt that the analyst not only attempts to describe the over-all effects of the reserve but he also attempts to separate the performances of the retail and the Fieldcrest divisions. Information of the latter nature will not be found in the Marshall Field annual reports.

---

[1]Colgate-Palmolive Peet Co., Annual Report, 1947, p. 6.

[2]J.K. Butters, Effects of Taxation: Inventory Accounting and Policies (Boston: Harvard University, 1949), p. 248.

B. MARSHALL FIELD EARNINGS PER COMMON SHARE; (After Preferred Dividends)

	Before Inventory Reserve Adjustment			After Inventory Reserve Adjustment*		
	Retail Div.	Field-crest	Total	Retail Div.	Field-crest	Total
1953	$2.60	$0.20	$2.80	$2.60	$0.20	$2.80
1952	2.03	0.01	2.04	2.38	0.18	2.56
1951	2.64	(0.15)	2.49	2.46	(0.23)	2.23
1950	3.68	1.07	4.75	2.89	0.68	3.57
1949	3.37	0.29	3.66	3.68	0.45	4.13

*Inventory Reserve Adjustment allocated 2/3 to retail division--1/3 to Fieldcrest. 1/3 of the company's total inventory reserve was allocated to Fieldcrest Mills at the time of its sale.

C. Discussion: While Fieldcrest Mills continually furnished from 16 per cent to 20 per cent of Field's total sales from 1946 through 1952 its contribution to operating profits was erratic. In 1948 and 1950, peak textile years, the mills accounted for more than 1/5 of total operating profits but since 1950 their contribution to profits has been negligible.

Viewed alone, the retail division shows a slow, steady growth in sales and fairly stable profit margins. The company does not use the LIFO method of inventory valuation. However, a reserve for inventory price declines is maintained and yearly adjustments are made to this reserve to reflect changes in merchandise prices during the year. Since the reserve is deducted from inventory on the balance sheet and adjustments of the reserve are charged or credited to net income the effects of inventory valuation on income are essentially the same as if the LIFO method were used. The fluctuations in operating margins as shown in the first table would be less severe if they had reflected adjustments to the inventory reserve.

The stabilizing effect on earnings from adjustments to the inventory reserve is shown clearly in the preceding table. For instance, during the period 1950 through 1953, there was a difference between high and lower share earnings of the retail division of $1.65 before reserve adjustment but only $0.51 after adjustment. These figures on a per share basis also show the erratic and unsatisfactory nature of Fieldcrest earnings since 1950.

Hazel-Atlas Glass

The following lengthy quotation from a written analysis of the Hazel Atlas Glass Company is reproduced completely because it illustrates the extent to which some analysts will delve into the accounting procedures of a company. The underlined portions of the analysis are my italics. The following points can be observed from the work of this analyst:

(a) The Hazel Atlas Glass Company is typical in that it has never released any information regarding specific debits and credits to the reserve.

(b) The analyst probes as best he can based on the facts which are available plus some of the more reasonable assumptions which can be made as a substitute for unknown information.

(c) Such areas as the intricate accounting procedures involving inventory reserves *are* investigated, even though their final importance may be negligible.

Hazel Atlas Finished Goods Inventory Reserve

I. PURPOSE: Discussion of the probable effects on earnings and financial position of the company by use of this reserve.

II. DESCRIPTION OF THE RESERVE

Part of the company's finished goods inventory is valued, for balance sheet purposes, on a LIFO type basis. These finished goods are carried on the balance sheet at various discounts from their lowest historical (i.e., depression of the 1930s) selling prices. The difference between these constant figures and the current cost of manufacture is charg into an inventory reserve, and the amount of the reserve is deducted from the cost of the finished goods so valued before that item is recorded on the published balance sheet.

Mr. McNash, President of Hazel Atlas, in talking with our representative in September of this year, stated that the finished goods inventory reserve is currently about equal to the balance sheet value of the finished goods inventory or approximately $2.8 million. He further stated that the inventory reserve is a tax-free reserve which means that no income tax liability has yet been incurred or paid on earnings which have been credited to this reserve.

The present accounting method for valuation of the finished goods inventory has been in effect at least since 1941.

The company has never released any information regarding specific credits and debits to the reserve.

III. PROBABLE EFFECTS CAUSED BY USE OF THE RESERVE

A. General Conclusions: Perhaps the only precise conclusion which can be drawn from the data available is that, if the reserve now equals $2.8 million, the company's pretax earnings have been understated by this amount over the period since the creation of the reserve. To what extent net earnings have been affected by the reserve depends on assumptions concerning the tax rates that would have been applied against the amounts credited to the reserve had they been left as pretax earnings. To what extent net earnings have been affected in any one year, or the extent to which use of the reserve has tended to reduce fluctuations in reported net earnings, depends on tax rate assumptions plus knowledge of the amounts which have been added to or subtracted from the reserve in each year since it was first established. The following discussion is not entirely based on known facts but on the facts that are available plus some of the more reasonable assumptions which can be made as a substitute for unknown information.

B. Effects on earnings using various assumptions: Changes in the stated value of the finished goods inventory can be computed from the balance sheets of the company. If it is assumed that these changes bear a positive relationship to changes in the reserve in the corresponding years, certain conclusions can be made as to the effect of the reserve on reported net earnings from year to year. The following table shows the changes in the balance sheet value of the finished goods inventory.

It is noted that the change in the balance sheet value of the finished goods inventory from 1941 to 1952 is a negative figure. Either the size of the reserve was smaller in 1952, than it was in 1941, or some change in accounting methods has taken place during this period.

The experience in the period 1946 to 1952 would seem to be the more reasonable one to use in extrapolating effects on reported net earnings from changes in the

Hazel Atlas Glass Company Changes in Balance Sheet Value of Finished Goods Inventory (Thousands)

	Finished Goods Inventory	Change from Previous Year	Cumulative from 1941	Cumulative from 1946
1941	$3,727	..	..	..
1942	2,252	-$1,475	-$1,475	..
1943	1,826	- 426	- 1,901	..
1944	2,410	+ 584	- 1,317	..
1945	1,869	- 541	- 1,858	..
1946	1,477	- 392	- 2,250	..
1947	2,291	+ 814	- 1,436	+ 814
1948	2,488	+ 197	- 1,239	+1,011
1949	2,762	+ 274	- 965	+1,285
1950	1,972	- 790	- 1,755	+ 495
1951	2,337	+ 365	- 1,390	+ 860
1952	2,847	+ 510	- 880	+1,370

balance sheet value of the finished goods inventory. Assuming a change in the balance sheet inventory figure to be equal to the change in the inventory reserve in a given year, the table below shows the effects on reported per share earnings for the years 1947 through 1952.

	Addition to Inventory Reserve	Equivalent Per Common Share	Applicable Tax Rate*	Equivalent Per Common Share After Taxes	Reported Earnings Per Common Share	Adjusted Earnings Per Common Share
1947	$ 814	$.37	38.4%	$ .23	$ 1.83	$ 2.06
1948	197	.09	38.8%	.06	1.41	1.47
1949	274	.13	37.5%	.08	1.83	1.91
1950	790	.36	42.8%	.21	1.66	1.45
1951	365	.17	54.0%	.08	1.55	1.63
1952	510	.23	46.4%	.12	1.36	1.48
Total	$1,370	$.63	42.9%	$.36	$ 9.64	$10.00

*Actual income tax rate incurred by Hazel Atlas in each year.

Using these assumptions $1.5 million is the net amount credited to the inventory reserve during this period. After taxes this represents an understatement of net income by thirty-six cents per share, or 3.7 per cent, during the six-year period. This would not seem to involve a significant distortion of earnings. Nor is any smoothing of the ups and downs of yearly reported earnings shown. The spread on yearly reported earnings from 1947 through 1952 is forty-seven cents or 35 per cent of the low year, while the spread on yearly adjusted earnings for the same period was sixty-one cents or 42 per cent of the low year. Moreover, the downward trend in earnings since 1947 is clearly visible in either set of figures. Under these conditions it would be assumed that $1.4 million had been credited to the inventory reserve in years previous to 1946.

If it were assumed the entire $2.8 million inventory reserve had been built up since 1946, this would represent about $1.29 per share before taxes. Using the average tax rate in the table above the reserve would equal seventy-six cents after taxes. Under these conditions, earnings during the six-year period would have been understated by about 7.9 per cent. Even under these extreme assumptions, it would not seem that earnings have been seriously understated over a period of years.

C. Effects on financial position: Essentially the operation of the finished goods inventory reserve results in an understatement of inventory and an understatement of earned surplus on the balance sheet. It does not affect the cash position unless and until a portion of the reserve is returned to the pretax income account, become subject to taxes, and thus tends to reduce cash holdings as tax payments are increased. In other words, it would seem that the existence of the inventory reserve, and additions to it at the expense of earnings, simply allows the company to avoid present incidence of Federal income taxes on the amount credited to the reserve.

The undervaluation of the finished goods inventory on the balance sheet is a plus factor in analyzing the company's financial position to the extent that it mitigates against a precipitate decline in inventory values in a period of rapidly declining prices. However, real assets have been increased only in the amount of income taxes avoided, and benefit to the stockholders from this must come from profitable investment of this asset increment.

Hercules Motors

Some companies use one basis of inventory valuation for the income tax return and another basis for reports to stockholders. When the lifo method is used for tax purposes there are no resulting inventory reserves and no related differences between reported and taxable income. But when the lifo result is obtained by setting up reserves, not recognized for tax purposes, a difference will be created. The following table illustrates what the analyst would do in such a case as Hercules Motors' 1947 earnings.[1]

	Tax Return (Fifo Basis)	Reported to Stockholders (Lifo without Tax Credit)	As Adjusted by the Analyst (True Lifo Basis)
Net before tax (fifo).	$3,341,000	$3,341,000	$3,341,000
Applicable tax	1,290,000	1,290,000	1,290,000
Life reserve (included in cost of sales . . .	..	dr. 849,000	dr.849,000
Less applicable tax credit.	..	..	cr.322,000
Net for common stock . . .	2,051,000	1,202,000	1,524,000
Per Share . .	$ 6.60	$ 3.87	$ 4.92

Stewart Warner

Stewart Warner presents a somewhat different problem. Like Hercules it pays income tax on a fifo basis but calculates its reported earnings on a lifo basis. But it adjusts its income account and balance sheet to reflect the tax credit related to the lifo deduction, thus presumably placing its final earnings on a true lifo basis. Nonetheless there are unexplained differences of considerable size between the reported earnings and the

[1]Graham and Dodd, op. cit., p. 167.

adjusted tax provision, as is shown below for 1948.[1]

	Indicated Tax Return (Fifo)	Reported to Stockholders (Lifo, Tax Adjusted)
Net before tax.	$ 7,447,000	$ 6,114,000
Income tax.	3,493,000	2,960,000
Net after tax	3,954,000	3,154,000
Net after tax indicated by tax provision	5,240,000	4,440,000
Difference unexplained. . .	1,286,000	1,286,000
Indicated profit per share.	Fifo basis	$ 4.00
	Lifo basis	3.42
Reported profit per share .	Lifo basis	2.44

National Lead

National Lead Company has a reputation of sorts among analysts as being a company with unusually conservative accounting policies. The following analysis of National Lead reflects the general attitude among analysts that inventory reserve procedures which keep inventory "profits" and "losses" out of the measurement of income are not desirable. This point is illustrated in the following analysis because the analyst emphasizes the recasting of the company's figures which "affords a reasonable accurate indication of results based on actual operations." There is a definite opinion that the company figures do not reflect "actual" results. This is reflected in the statement below which says, "This adjustment shows that earnings are more unstable than reported figures have indicated." The underlined passages are my italics.

[1]Graham and Dodd, *op. cit.*, pp. 167-168.

National Lead Company

5. Accounting Methods: Accounting methods followed by the company are unusually conservative. All foreign holdings including antimony mines in Mexico, fabricating plants in Argentina, extensive manufacturing and distributing facilities in Canada and England, ilmenite mines in Norway, and titanium pigment plants in Germany (which would cost $50 million to reproduce in the U.S.), have been written off.

The method of valuation of inventories is equally conservative and is based on the "normal stock" system which was adopted about 1915. For this purpose the essential raw materials (lead, tin, antimony and linseed oil) are divided into "normal stock" and stock in excess of normal. The normal stock is valued at the lowest price reached in 1932. Stocks in excess of normal are valued at the lower of cost or market. No profits or losses on the normal stock are reported to the stockholders.

The following table shows that at 12-31-51 the market price ($23,905,000) of the normal stock inventory exceeded the fixed price valuation ($3,905,000) by $20 million, which was about $5 million more than the inventory reserve at that time. However, recent softness of metal prices has decreased the market value of the normal stock to $20,882,160 (as of 8-12-52). Thus the current market valuation of $20,882,160 is only moderately higher than the fixed price valuation of $3,905,000 plus the inventory reserve of $15,011,777. The significance of this fact is that the company may not feel impelled to add to inventory reserves this year if the price of metals remains at current levels. Thus higher earnings may be reported.

	Normal Quantities (Short Tons)	Fixed Inventory--Price Per Pound	Normal Quantites Times Fixed Prices	12-31-51 Market Prices Per Lb.	Normal Quantities Times 12-31-51 Market Prices	Normal Quantities Times 8-12-52 Market Prices*
Lead. . . .	49,688	$0.03	$2,918,000	$0.19	$18,850,000	$15,900,160
Tin	1,125	0.21	472,000	1.03	2,320,000	2,733,750
Antimony. .	1,400	0.05	140,000	0.50	1,400,000	1,092,000
Linseed Oil	3,125	0.06	375,000	0.21	1,335,000	1,156,250
			$3,905,000		$23,905,000	$20,882,160

*Price per pound: Lead, $0.16; Tin, $1.215; Antimony, $0.39; and Linseed Oil, $0.185.

Because of National Lead's extensive use of reserves, including inventory reserves described above, in its accounting system, the reported income figures tend to be overstated in years in which lead prices are declining and understated in which lead prices are rising. It is believed a restatement of earnings for the years 1937 to 1951 affords a reasonably accurate indication of results based on actual operations.

According to our adjusted net income figures, the company's earnings as reported since 1937, have been understated by approximately $26.3 million. This adjustment shows that earnings are more unstable than reported figures have indicated. For example, in 1948 the company reported net income of $13.3 millions or $1.15 per share, not including $5.8 million set aside for inventory reserves. After adding back the reserves and other charges we find the actual results to have been $19.6 million, or $1.71 a share. However, in 1949 $10.1 million was taken from the inventory reserve and added to net income. This was partially offset by $4.1 million of nonrecurrent charges. Thus 1949 reported earnings were both overstated and understated, but the adjusted earnings were $0.78 a share contrasted with the $1.29 reported.

Additional earning capacity not reflected in the consolidated statement is represented by National Lead's equity in the undistributed earnings of foreign subsidiaries and partially-owned domestic companies. These earnings (not included in the consolidated report) have amounted to approximately 8.5 per cent of reported earnings since 1937 as shown below:

National Lead Company

	1951	1950	1949	1948	1947	1946	Average 1937-1945
Net income as reported	$2.05	$2.41	$1.29	$1.15	$1.04	$0.78	$0.40
Equity in undivided profits	0.09	0.03	0.09	0.15	0.10	0.02	0.05

Summary

It has already been emphasized that financial analysts are the major consumers of the published data issued by management with the aid of accountants. One of the salient considerations which always should be remembered by the drafters of annual reports is that the analyst is faced with the task of comparison of results between years and between similar firms. The analyst is not so unsophisticated that he thinks all firms in all industries should be forced to adopt inflexible accounting policies and rigid uniformity. But he realistically desires sufficient information so that he might carry out his task of comparison without the need for his making arbitrary assumptions concerning a firm's accounting procedures or key amounts charged or credited to particular accounts.[1]

The first paramount consideration which flows from the presentation in this chapter is simply that the revealing of the mere basis of valuation is not adequate disclosure. The nature of each of the bases of inventory valuation differs markedly with the method and procedure used and the segment of the inventories with which it is concerned. Inventory figures, like so many other figures in accounting, are general, pliable estimates. The figure which appears in the financial statements is only one of several alternative dollar values attributable to the quantities in the inventory.

From the analyst's point of view, then, it seems that the minimum requirements for disclosure with respect to inventories would embrace the following essentials:

1. There should be "cautious applications of terminology."[2]
2. Inventories should be broken down by major classes, by dollar amounts, and by methods of valuation.

---

[1]For an example of such efforts see the Hazel Atlas analysis (<u>supra</u>).

[2]William J. Vatter, "Limitations of Overhead Allocation," <u>Accounting Review</u>, XX, No. 2 (April, 1945), 176.

3. There should be a brief description of the details of the valuation methods employed.
4. Where feasible, physical quantities should also be disclosed. In this way price and quantity analysis may be facilitated. Several analysts expressed special desire for disclosure of physical quantities.
5. Where last-in, first-out, base-stock, and similar methods of valuation are used, an estimate of current replacement cost should be disclosed.
6. Where inventory reserves are used, full disclosure of the following points is desirable:
   (a) Their origin (whether the reserves arose out of an accounting entry debiting expense or one debiting retained earnings).
   (b) Their purpose and function.
   (c) Whether they are essentially asset valuation accounts, liabilities, or retained earnings.
   (d) Disclosure of the specific amounts debited and credited to the reserves each year.

The application of the above standards of disclosure plus consistent adherence to a given method and procedure of inventory valuation should give the analyst ample opportunity to make any adjusting calculations he feels are necessary in order to develop comparability between companies.

CHAPTER VI

NON-RECURRING ITEMS

This phase of the study is concerned with the financial reporting of non-recurring items: that is, those items which are not likely to appear in a corporate income statement year after year. Examples of non-recurring items include gains or losses on disposals of securities and fixed assets; items arising from the carry-forward and carry-back provisions of the federal income tax laws; "losses" from flood, fire, and other disasters, losses from law suits; and corrections of accounting errors applicable to past periods. Special problems in regard to such items do not arise unless the amounts involved are material. But material non-recurring items have appeared often enough so that the financial presentation of these items has become a major issue in accounting and financial circles.[1]

This chapter is divided into four parts. The first part presents the analysts' views with respect to non-recurring items.

---

[1]"Material" amounts mean different things to different persons. For the purpose of this discussion a "material" amount is one which affects the net result by more than 10 per cent. James L. Dohr, "Materiality--What Does It Mean in Accounting?" Journal of Accountancy, XC, No. 1 (July, 1950), 56, offers the following definition of materiality: "A statement, fact, or item is material, if, giving full consideration to the surrounding circumstances, as they exist at the time, it is of such a nature that its disclosure, or the method of treating it, would be likely to influence or to "make a difference' in the judgment and conduct of a reasonable person."

The second part presents the accountants' views. The third part discusses the handling of income taxes as an example of the problem. The fourth part attempts to draw conclusions concerning the existing divergent views.

Analysts' Views

Analysts' views concerning non-recurring items have been expressed often and in many places. Apparently there is one point of view, and that is that non-recurring items should be excluded in the determination of net income. Probably the most convincing exposition of their views can be presented by directly quoting expressions of the analysts' attitudes.

The words of E. Linwood Savage, Jr., Chairman of the Committee on Corporate Information of the National Federation of Financial Analysts serve suitably as the keynote for the discussion which follows:

> My second major point pertaining to financial statements (his first major point was a plea for greater uniformity within industries) involves the controversial "all-inclusive" income account. The "all-inclusive" theory holds that all profit-and-loss items should be reported in the income account and implies that management has no obligation to present a "net income figure" which represents the results of "normal" as distinguished from "non-recurring" operations, during the year. In our judgment this theory fails to recognize the overwhelming emphasis placed on the one income-account item, "net income," because of the practical necessity of using one figure to represent the year's results, especially by news-gathering and statistical services.
>
> Corporate management, with the aid of public accountants, is unquestionably in the best position to determine what may be regarded as "nonrecurring." Because of the importance placed on the single figure "net income," management should do its best to see that "non-recurring" items are not allowed to affect this figure. We agree that "nonrecurring" items should be included, but their place is below the "net income" line rather than above it.
>
> A simple example of what I have in mind is the 1951 report of the Kroger Company, which included the proceeds of the sale of fixed assets in computing "net income." This inclusion increased net 39 per cent, and, although no analyst would

> regard the resulting figure as representing Kroger's results for the year, it was picked up and quoted by the statistical services as such. It is their regular practice to use whatever figure is reported as "net income" in their releases, which is the stuff that statistical manuals are made of later; you will find the inflated figure in the latest Moody's Industrial Manual labeled "net income."[1]

Another analyst expressed his opinion in the following manner:

> It is vital that the published earnings, as shown by a corporation's accounts, reflect the true earning power, consistently and clearly presented, rather than a higher or lower figure resulting from extraordinary credits or charges. . . .
>
> Charges and credits of an extraordinary nature may well be revealed in a presentation of the surplus account, reconciling the surplus figure at the end of the prior year with that for the year just reviewed. The surplus adjustments should be stated clearly enough to enable the analyst to decide whether or not, in his judgment, the items so charged or credited are truly inapplicable to the year under examination. I have in mind such items as profits or losses from the sale of securities or the sale of capital assets. These can scarcely be regarded as operating profits or losses applicable to the year in which they are taken. From the analyst's viewpoint, it seems logical, therefore, to omit them from the income account and include them in the reconciliation of surplus. If unusual charges are made to reserve accounts, such as the contingency reserve account, a statement of changes in the reserve account should also be given.[2]

The 1953 report of the Committee on Corporate Information of the National Federation of Financial Analysts in referring to the oil companies expressed the desire to have companies report earnings per share excluding nonrecurring income and expense items.[3]

---

[1] E. Linwood Savage, Jr., "Conclusions Regarding Annual Reports," The Analysts Journal, X, No. 1 (February, 1954), 51.

[2] Dwight P. Robinson, Jr., "Accountants' Reports and Audited Accounts from an Investment Analyst's Viewpoint," Journal of Accountancy, LXVII, No. 2 (February, 1939), 81.

[3] Committee on Corporate Information, National Federation of Financial Analysts Societies, "Reports of National Committees for 1953," (New York; New York Society of Security Analysts, Inc., 1954), p. 15.

The Committee on Corporate Information is currently surveying annual reports of the aircraft industry. One of the Committee's major recommendations will be as follows:

> Present a net income figure representing results of the manufacturing operations as distinct from any unusual and non-recurring transaction. The effect of extraordinary and non-recurring income and expense items which must be included in the year's statement of income should be detailed, with the net income figure on a per share basis presented exclusive of such items. The importance of this cannot be over-estimated as the financial services report a per share figure which a company releases, generally without the necessary supplemental information which would segregate extraordinary and non-recurring items.[1]

Graham and Dodd offer the following observations:

> Most of the non-recurrent items play a double and contradictory role in security analysis. They should be excluded in arriving at the results for a single year, but they should be included in the over-all results for a period of years. A substantial refund of overpaid taxes, for example, has nothing to do with the year's operating profit, and it is a misuse of language to call it part of the "earnings" of the year in which it was received.[2]

The specific stand which Graham and Dodd take on the matter of non-recurring items is outlined below:

> 1. Small items should be accepted as reported. . . .
> 2. When a large item is excluded, a corresponding adjustment must be allowed for in the income tax deduction.
> 3. Most non-recurrent items excluded from the single year's analysis must nevertheless be included in a statement of long-term or average results.[3]

Another analyst, J.M. Galanis, whose article has received widespread approval among fellow analysts, expressed the following opinion:

---

[1]Committee on Corporate Information, National Federation of Financial Analysts Societies, "Aircraft Industry Annual Reporting--1953," (unpublished mimeographed report, dated April 7, 1954), p. 2.

[2]B. Graham and D. Dodd, Security Analysis (3rd ed.; New York: McGraw Hill, Inc., 1951), pp. 89-90.

[3]*Ibid.*, p. 90.

> It is especially important that nonrecurring items be shown separately and clearly. This applies particularly to gains (or losses) from sales of fixed assets where such transactions are cleared through the income rather than the surplus account. The analyst would greatly prefer to see all gains or losses from sales of fixed assets and tax transactions resulting therefrom handled through the surplus rather than the income account; otherwise, earnings are distorted and year to year and company to company comparisons are made meaningless. . . .
>
> By separate treatment in the income account of all special and nonoperating items of this character, distortions can be eliminated and calculation of pretax margins of profit can be made that more nearly reflect the true and dependable (or "normal") earning power of enterprise.[1]

The analysts' views are distinctly summarized by one analyst as follows:

> I was particularly interested in his [Galanis] comments on the importance of showing nonrecurring income items separately and clearly.
>
> These comments, which I believe express the opinion of the great majority of, if not all, security analysts, are particularly timely in view of the recently published Bulletin 32 of the American Institute of Accountants.
>
> I . . . would like to see the Society of Security Analysts take a definite stand favoring an income statement which definitely excludes from the published "net income," or "net income per share" figure, all nonrecurring and other items, which do not reflect the ordinary year's operations.[2]

The above quotations have been supported in this writer's conversations with analysts. All of the analysts seek a measure of earning power, and all of them indicate that the best available basis as a single measure was net income excluding non-recurring items.

---

[1] J.M. Galanis, "Shortcomings of Financial Statements from the Security Analyst's Viewpoint," Analysts Journal, III, No. 4 (November, 1947), 38-39.

[2] Gearhead G. Sturm, Goldman, Sachs and Co., "Letter to the Editor," Analysts Journal, IV, No. 2 (April, 1948), 35-36.

Accountants' Views

The problems of periodic income determination offer difficulties which are, practically speaking, irreconcilable. Hatfield commented:

> Nine-tenths of the problems of the accountant are due to this demand to express results in terms of years. The accountant is wrestling with it. That it has not been solved is apparent to anyone who opens a text on the subject, or who enters into the intricacies of the income tax.[1]

Allowing for the moment the myriad of inventory and depreciation methods, accounting conventions have yielded a fairly uniform presentation which has little, if any, uniformity even within the same company over a short period of years.[2]

The citing of the importance of periodic net income is included in the American Institute of Accountants' summary of its research bulletins:

> The problems in the field of accounting have increasingly come to be considered from the standpoint of the buyer or seller of an interest in an enterprise, with consequent increased recognition of the significance of the income statement and a tendency to restrict narrowly charges and credits to surplus. The fairest possible presentation of periodic net income, with neither material overstatement nor understatement, is important, since the results of operations are significant not only to prospective buyers of an interest in the enterprise but also to prospective sellers. With the increasing importance of the income statement there has been a tendency to regard the balance sheet as the connecting link between successive income statements; however this concept should not obscure the fact that the balance sheet has significant uses of its own.[3]

---

[1] Henry Rand Hatfield, "An Historical Defense of Bookkeeping," reprinted in The Illinois Certified Public Accountant, XV, No. 4 (June, 1953), 41.

[2] For an illustration of inconsistent treatment of taxes by a firm, see the example of Endicott Johnson Corporation in Graham and Dodd, op. cit., pp. 115-116.

[3] Committee on Accounting Procedure, American Institute of Accountants, Accounting Research Bulletin No. 43: Restatement and Revision of Accounting Research Bulletins (New York: American Institute of Accountants, 1953), p. 7.

A leading supporter of a "sharp" net income (instead of an "all-inclusive" figure which includes non-recurring items), George D. Bailey, has commented:

> It seems to me that the need for a sharp determination of income of a corporation for a given year is so great as to override any advantage of the all-inclusive income statement in having all items which are "bookkeeped" during the year shown in one statement--and to override any contention that orderly accounting requires that items get into the surplus account only by means of the income statement. The income statement must be as sharp a presentation of corporate income for the year as it is possible to make it. . . .
>
> . . . Responsibility is on the issuing corporation and on its public accountants to interpret the items for the reader, and to segregate those items which affect the income for the year from those which are not to be considered in judging the efficiency of operations for the year. . . .
>
> Perhaps the philosophy of the corporate income statement as developed here can be stated as follows:
>
> (1) the presentation of corporate income must be developed to have the maximum usefulness for "non-insiders."
>
> (2) Such emphasis puts the responsibility on the management and on the accountant for proper analysis of the statement to show clearly the net income for the year.
>
> (3) The net income for the year must be shown as sharply as possible in order to make the statements useful in forming opinions as to the efficiency of the company and permit making decisions affecting the future.
>
> (4) The income statements must be considered in the light of the economic conditions of the year for which they are presented, and bookkeeping items which cushion the impact of those economic conditions should not be included in the determination of income.
>
> (5) The variety of practice must be reduced, an orderly body of accounting principles extended, and criteria established against which accounting judgment may be tested, to the end that statements of different companies may be satisfactorily compared.[1]

Many leading accountants feel strongly that the problems of corporate reporting would best be solved by the "all-inclusive" approach to the income statement. The proponents of this method of determining and presenting income maintain that all elements of revenue and expense and losses and extraordinary or

---

[1]George D. Bailey, "The Increasing Significance of the Income Statement," Journal of Accountancy, LXXXV, No. 1 (January, 1948), 10-11.

items should be included in determining net income for the year.[1] That is, the "net income" figure is shown after corrections relating to past years' operations and all other non-recurring items have been considered in calculations. Spokesmen for the American Accounting Association have endorsed this position as follows:

> The income of an accounting period should be reported in a statement providing an exhibit of all revenue and expense (including losses) given accounting recognition during that period. This practice assures that the income statements for a period of years will disclose completely the entire income history of that period.[2]

The all-inclusive approach is a step that evolved from an attempt to eliminate past abuses of using the surplus statement and surplus reserve accounts to relieve the income statement of appropriate items.[3] But the question remains as to whether the all-inclusive remedy which has been suggested is the best remedy available. As Paton, an all-inclusive adherent, so aptly pointed

---

[1]For an extended exposition of the pros and cons of the all-inclusive approach see H.A. Finney and H.E. Miller, Principles of Accounting--Intermediate (4th ed.; New York: Prentice Hall, Inc., 1951), pp. 111-113.

[2]Executive Committee, American Accounting Association, "Accounting Concepts and Standards Underlying Corporate Financial Statements," Accounting Review, XXIII, No. 4 (October, 1948), 343 and sections on "Income" and "expense," pp. 340-341.

[3]William Werntz, as chief accountant for the S.E.C., "The Income Statement," in Termination and Taxes (New York: American Institute of Accountants, 1944), p. 162, observed: "Emphasis of an 'earning capacity' figure which by hypothesis excludes the effects of such items glosses over one of the major limitations of the accounting process and in the long run may bring it into disrepute. The barest reference to the accounting practices of earlier years will call to mind almost innumerable cases in which earnings were reported year after year by companies which never seemed to be able to pay dividends or to accumulate an earned surplus. And there will continue to be such situations as long as accountants are liberal in excluding items from the income statement and support propositions such as these: that prospective losses on investments and long-term assets need be given no current recognition whatever and that any realized losses on sale of such assets may go to surplus because they are 'unusual' or are allocable to past years.'"

out, "The primary function of accounting is to furnish significant, useful information to managers and owners of business enterprises regarding assets, liabilities, revenues. . . ."[1] Paton feels that the all-inclusive statement is the best vehicle by which useful information can be supplied.

However, many accountants feel that the all-inclusive income statement falls short of meeting the test of furnishing significant, useful information. An editorial in the Journal of Accountancy points out some difficulties:

> But it [the all-inclusive statement] had the disadvantage of compelling readers of financial statements, often unskilled in accounting, to judge for themselves the significance of extraordinary transactions, adjustments, reserves, and the like, in attempting to appraise the effectiveness with which the regular operations of the business were conducted. Mr. Bailey says that management and its independent auditors should assume that responsibility. His contention gains strength from the tendency to cite a single figure of "profit," or earnings per share, as an indication of the value of securities, or the ability of a company to raise wages or lower prices.[2]

The Securities and Exchange Commission has strongly supported the all-inclusive approach. Except as otherwise permitted, the Commission currently requires that: "All items of profit and loss given recognition in the accounts during the period covered by the profit and loss or income statements shall be included.[3]

However, it is noteworthy that the Commission advocates

---

[1] W.A. Paton, in Blough et al., "Restoration of Fixed Asset Values to the Balance Sheet," Accounting Review, XXII, No. 2 (April, 1947), 199.

[2] Editorial, Journal of Accountancy, LXXXV, No. 1 (January, 1948), 2.

[3] Securities and Exchange Commission, Regulation S-X (Washington, D.C.: U.S. Government Printing Office, 1951), Rule 5.03 (a), p. 20. Also see S.E.C., Fourteenth Annual Report (Washington, D.C.: U.S. Government Printing Office, 1948), p. 111.

that, after the net income figure is drawn, "special items" shall be appended and a final figure called "net income and special items" shall be shown.[1] Thus apparently the Commission favors a "net income" figure that is not all-inclusive but an income statement that is all-inclusive.

A pertinent observation with respect to this controversy follows:

> The [American Accounting] Association, representing the academic world, is sincere and objective, beyond question, and its position can be referred to by those who prefer the easier way, because it is easier beyond doubt for corporations, for accountants, for government regulatory bodies, and for the S.E.C. to have everything treated before determining an income figure . . . than it is to assume the difficult responsibility of excluding extraordinary and material transactions not related to the year's operations, a task involving accounting knowledge, integrity, and independence of the highest order. Certainly the acceptance of the all-inclusive theory would make for an easier, even though not a more useful, profession of accounting.[2]

Thus the yearly determination of net income revolves around a fundamental issue: which of the concepts of net income will be the most useful for the most people. Certainly everyone cannot be satisfied. And it seems that usefulness for the investor is the paramount consideration. Benjamin Graham maintains, "Prospective earnings are, basically, the most important thing that the analyst must consider in a typical case."[3]

The weight of analysts' opinions has been heavily inclined toward favoring a sharp net income figure. Yet the Securities and

---

[1] Ibid., Rule 5.03 (c) 17, p. 21.

[2] George D. Bailey, "Problems in Reporting Corporation Income," Harvard Business Review, XXVI, No. 5 (September, 1948), 682-683.

[3] B.J. Graham, "Financial Statements from the Viewpoint of the Financial Analyst," New York Certified Public Accountant, XV, No. 5 (May, 1945), 232.

Exchange Commission, the governmental watchdog for investors, has definitely supported the all-inclusive approach.

The Committee on Accounting Procedure of the American Institute of Accountants has endorsed the sharp income statement approach and has attempted to draft criteria for use in determining how material nonrecurring items should be handled.[1]

The conflicting views of the above experts point toward the web of weaknesses that is weaved by the net income concept. William Vatter's comment in this regard deserves emphasis:

---

[1]Committee on Accounting Procedure, op. cit., pp. 59-65. A summary of the Committee's position is found on p. 63 as follows:

"1. The Committee has indicated elsewhere that in its opinion it is plainly desirable that over the years all profits and losses of a business be reflected in net income, but at the same time has recognized that, under appropriate circumstances, it is proper to exclude certain material charges and credits from the determination of the net income of a single year, even though they clearly affect the cumulative total of income for a series of years. In harmony with this view, it is the opinion of the committee that there should be a general presumption that all items of profit and loss recognized during the period are to be used in determining the figure reported as net income. The only possible exception to this presumption related to items which in the aggregate are material in relation to the company's net income and are clearly not identifiable with or do not result from the usual or typical business operations of the period. Thus, only extraordinary items such as the following may be excluded from the determination of net income for the year, and they should be excluded when their inclusion would impair the significance of net income so that misleading inferences might be drawn therefrom:

(a) Material charges or credits (other than ordinary adjustments of a recurring nature) specifically related to operations of prior years, such as the elimination of unused reserves provided in prior years and adjustments of income taxes for prior years:

(b) Material charges or credits resulting from unusual sales of assets not acquired for resale and not of the type in which the company generally deals;

(c) Material losses of a type not usually insured against, such as those resulting from wars, riots, earthquakes, and similar calamities or catastrophes except where such losses are of a recurrent hazard of the business;

(d) The write-off of a material amount of intangibles;

(e) The write-off of material amounts of unamortized bond discount or premium and bond issue expenses at the time of the retirement or refunding of the debt before maturity."

As it is, the most realistic statement that can be made about the income figure so prominently displayed in the reports is the statement made by Canning: "What is set out as a measure of net income can never be supposed to be a fact in any sense at all except that it is the figure which results when the accountant has finished applying the procedure which he adopts."[1]

Income Taxes

As already mentioned, the section of the income statement which follows the operating margin before income taxes and non-recurring items is the one in which there is the greatest lack of uniformity and the greatest difference of opinion as to proper presentation and disclosure.[2] In this respect the presentation of income taxes is undoubtedly the most important issue of the moment.[3] In recent years the intricate provisions of the income and excess profits taxes have had a weighty impact upon corporate reporting. First, the amounts involved are significant. Second, the carry-back and carry-forward provisions, the claims for refunds, and the "sharp" or "normal" income notion have generated clashing opinions with regard to correct treatment.

Institute opinion has not been in agreement with S.E.C. opinion. The matter of presenting income taxes is handled in widely varying fashions in annual reports.[4]

---

[1]W.J. Vatter, The Fund Theory of Accounting and Its Implications for Financial Reports (Chicago: University of Chicago Press, 1947), p. 76.

[2]W.P. Trumbull, "The All-Inclusive Standard," Accounting Review, XXVII, No. 1 (January, 1952), 7-8, cites specific examples of how firms differ in the handling of prior-year tax adjustments.

[3]Footnotes to the income statements often provide sufficient information with regard to income taxes. For examples see B.B. Greidinger, Preparation and Certification of Financial Statements (New York: Ronald Press Co., 1950), p. 292.

[4]Research Department of the American Institute of Accountants, Accounting Trends and Techniques, 1953 edition (New York:

Analysts' Views

The Committee on Corporate Information of the National Federation of Financial Analysts has formally recommended disclosure of the following with reference to the presentation of income taxes:

> 5. The amount of income on which income tax was computed and an explanation of any significant differences between income for tax purposes and income as reported to stockholders. In addition, the amount of Federal income tax and Federal excess profit tax should be stated as separate items.[1]

Graham and Dodd offer the following suggestions:

> Companies should be required to segregate in the income account not only all nonrecurrent items of any magnitude, but also the tax debit or credit related thereto. They should also be required to compute the earnings per share on the basis of ordinary income, excluding nonrecurrent items and their related tax.[2]

Being consistent with their "sharp" income views, analysts generally desire an allocation of income taxes between operating items and non-recurring items because they feel that it facilitate their work of measuring prospective earning power.[3] By taking

---

American Institute of Accountants, 1953), pp. 206-207, yields the following indication of varying practices:

Number of Companies Presenting Allocation of Income Taxes for Extraordinary Items:

Adjusting "income for the year"	34
Adjusting "income for the year and retained earnings account".	22
Adjusting "retained earnings account"	15
	51
Number of Companies not presenting allocation of income taxes for extraordinary items.	211
Number of Companies not presenting extraordinary items	338
	600

[1]Committee on Corporate Information, National Federation of Financial Analysts Societies, "Fourth Annual Report," The Analysts Journal, VIII, No. 4 (August, 1952), 216.

[2]B. Graham and D. Dodd, op. cit., p. 173.

[3]Committee on Corporate Information, "Fourth Annual

operating margin before taxes together with the tax amount which they feel is pertinent to such a margin, analysts believe that they can obtain a better measure of after-tax earning-power. But nevertheless, in addition, analysts want to know the actual amounts of normal income taxes plus excess profits taxes (when in effect).[1]

Institute's Views

The American Institute of Accountants' opinions on this matter tend to agree with the analysts' views in all important respects. The Institute Committee on Accounting Procedure has

---

Report," op. cit., p. 216, in referring to the annual reports of banks stated: "The income account should include recurring income and expense items only, and the income taxes deducted in arriving at net operating earnings should be applicable to those items only. Nonrecurring items such as profits and losses on investments, charge-offs, and recoveries should be reported as nonoperating items against which the income taxes or tax savings related to them should be shown."

[1]Benjamin Graham, "Financial Statements from the View-point of the Financial Analyst," New York Certified Public Accountant, XV, No. 5 (May, 1945), 236, offers an example of the analyst's thinking with respect to income tax reporting as follows:

"If you take the Gulf, Mobile and Ohio Railroad, you will find that they reported earnings in 1943 of $4.63 per share; but in a footnote they say that their taxes were reduced by the equivalent of $2.18 a share by reason of loss on property sold and various other special surplus adjustments. It is obvious that on the basis of their operations alone they would have been subject to much higher taxes, and the earnings would have been only $2.45 a share instead of $4.63--a very substantial difference.

"Now take, by way of contrast, the Twin City Rapid Transit Company. Its report for 1944 showed that they charged to income $2,120,000 of taxes: but they credited to surplus $543,000 of taxes, which was money saved because of debt retirement expense. In other words, they did not follow the Gulf, Mobile and Ohio procedure; instead they charged income with more than they actually paid for the year because they considered--quite properly--that the saving of taxes applicable to amounts charged to surplus should go directly into surplus and should not be credited to income. They have exactly the opposite picture from that of G.M. and O.; they showed earnings of $2.63 in their income account, but if they had followed the same procedure as Gulf, Mobile and Ohio, their earnings would have been $4.68 per share."

taken the following position:

> Income taxes are an expense that should be allocated, when necessary and practicable to income and other accounts, as other expenses are allocated. . . . The difficulties encountered in allocation of the tax are not greater than those met with in many other allocations of expenses. . . . In the committee's view, all that is necessary in making an allocation is to consider the effect on taxes of those special transactions which are not included in the income statement (materia non-recurring items).[1]

The Committee advocates that the portion of the provision for income taxes which is attributable to a material non-recurring item should be charged or credited against surplus if the item itself is cleared through surplus. Consequently, the provision for income taxes which appears on the income statement should be adjusted accordingly and thus would not represent the amount actually paid or payable for the year.[2]

Thus the Committee maintains that it is necessary to "allocate" the actual taxes between charges to surplus and income from operations, even if such a practice results in the inclusion in the income statement of a charge in excess of actual taxes payable, with an offsetting "credit" or "debit" being carried to surplus in an amount sufficient to reduce the charge for income taxes to the amount actually payable.

By allocating income taxes in the above manner, the Committee feels that the income statement becomes more useful to investors since it is more nearly indicative of "normal" conditions and probable results in the future.[3]

---

[1]Committee on Accounting Procedure, op. cit., p. 88.

[2]Ibid., pp. 88-92. [3]Ibid., p. 88.

Summary of Opposing Views

As can be seen from the table below, "all-inclusive" adherents tend to maintain that non-recurring items (before tax considerations) should follow the operating margin; then the income taxes actually paid or payable should be deducted in arriving at "net income" for the year.

Analysts generally prefer that the current amount of income taxes which would be paid on the operating margin should follow the latter. Following this, the non-recurring items should be appended together with their income tax effects. The resulting figure could be called "net income and non-recurring items."

More specifically, the alternative treatments are shown below in tabular form:

"All-Inclusive" Approach

Operating margin before income taxes and non-recurring items	$ xxx
Add or deduct non-recurring items	xxx
Margin after deducting non-recurring items. . . .	$ xxx
Provision for income taxes (actual amount paid or payable).	xxx
Net income.	$ xxx

Analyst's Approach

Operating margin before income taxes and non-recurring items	$ xxx
Income tax on above amount.	xxx
Operating margin after taxes (net income)	$ xxx
Non-recurring items (in detail)	xxx
Income tax (debit) or credit against non-recurring items	xxx
Net income and non-recurring items.	$ xxx

Allocation of Income Taxes

The issue with regard to income taxes really is not whether or not income taxes should be allocated. Accountingwise, "allocation" carries three separate meanings.[1] Basically, the issue lies in the choice of one of the two general methods of reporting. Should income taxes be deducted from income of the current year in the amount actually payable as taxes? Or should income taxes be prorated in the manner advocated by the Institute?

The Institute Committee urges that income taxes are an expense that should be allocated as other expenses are allocated. But the Committee does not attempt to explain why income taxes must be considered in the same category, as, for example, salaries. It is obvious the income taxes are a component of taxable net income. Unlike most expenses they exist only if there is net taxable income before any deduction for such taxes. Thus in a sense income taxes are a share of profits distributed to the government. Income taxes are a unique type of expense, one that is incurred only if net taxable income exists.

Furthermore it is important to remember that no expense other than income taxes is allocated by "applying to a given transaction much of the expense as would not have occurred if the transaction to which the expense is attributed had not taken place. The usual method is to allocate a total expense ratable

---

[1]Eric L. Kohler, A Dictionary for Accountants (New York: Prentice-Hall, Inc., 1952), offers the following definitions of the word "allocate":

"1. To charge an item or group of items of revenue or cost to an object, activity, process, operation, or product, in accordance with cost responsibilities, benefits received, or other measure of apportionment. Examples: To charge the amount of a voucher to an expense account; to spread fire-insurance-premium costs to departments in proportion to the insurable values of the assets located in such departments.

2. To distribute the total cost of a lump-sum purchase over the items purchased.

3. (governmental accounting) To transfer, by superior administrative authority, an appropriation or a part thereof from one agency to another."

to given accounts or transactions on a consistent basis."[1]

Ordinary expenses are usually distributed over a number of accounts on one or more of the following bases: units produced, measures of input, measures of time, or measures of benefits received. What the expense might have been under different conditions is regarded as irrelevant. Never is there a distribution of an expense to several accounts in which a negative sum is credited against one item to offset the positive amount charged to another item in excess of the actual expense. It is doubtful that such an approach enhances the meaning or usefulness of financial statements, if the latter are supposed to reflect the actual results of operations.

Certainly the "tax savings" factor looms large in many managerial decisions.[2] In support of the Institute's position it might be argued that "tax savings" must be allocated to particular losses or expenses because the tax consequences were an important decision-making factor. It could be claimed that, without the "tax saving," the securities or fixed assets would not have been sold. The "true" loss on the transaction is not the difference between cost and selling price but is equal to that difference offset by the "tax saving."[3] But why should non-

---

[1] Securities and Exchange Commission, Accounting Series Releases (Washington, D.C.: U.S. Government Printing Office, 1948), Release No. 53, p. 151.

[2] For case studies of the influences of income taxes on decision-making see W.J. Vatter, Management Planning for Corporate Taxes (New York: Controllership Foundation, Inc., 1951).

[3] Werntz, op. cit., pp. 162-163, made the following important observations: "How then can one adamantly say that a tax saving is attributable to the loss? Why not say a good deal more simply and, I think, logically, that an unusual loss was taken at a time when profits were unusually large? What is wrong or misleading or unrealistic in netting the two and showing the tax as levied on the balance? It seems to me that only on the basis of

recurring transactions be segregated for such treatment? Why not apply the same type of analysis to recurring operating decisions such as problems involving wages, advertising, bonuses, pensions, and inventory valuation procedures? Tax consequences often play an important role in these decisions also. Why not report wages and advertising as less in amount because income taxes would have been higher if the amounts spent on such items were less? The latter argument would be exploded by the well-grounded assertion that actual results would not be recorded and reported.

Thus there appears to be only a conjectural basis for adopting a special approach in arriving at a non-recurring result, such as the loss upon a sale of securities or fixed assets. The loss is the total difference between cost and selling price. The tax benefit is appropriately reflected in the lower taxes actually payable. The Institute's proposal tends to cloud the facts instead of clearly delineating what has taken place. If the taxes payable for a certain year are unusual in amount because of unusual conditions, an appropriate explanation should be forthcoming.

There are several additional criticisms that pertain to the Institute's position on allocation of income taxes. The determination of the amounts of the income tax applicable to particular non-recurring items is permeated with troublesome

---

many arbitrary assumptions can we pull apart the skein of the year's activities and events so as to isolate a particular transaction and say with assurance 'here is something that had no relation to the rest of the year's activities and can be excluded.' Particularly today it seems to me that we might well think about taxes and the so-called tax savings somewhat as follows: 'This year's revenues are unusual; this year's profits are unusual; this year's tax rates are unusual; as a result an unusual loss or transaction was put through and there results an unusual tax savings due to unusual tax rates due to the unusual profits of an unusual year.'"

difficulties. It is recommended by the Institute and it is generally accepted that the proposed transaction be treated as a marginal item when considering the impact of income taxes.[1] But is such a principle realistic when applied to the over-all operations for a year? Net taxable income is the difference between all taxable income and all deductible items applicable to the period. Picking out any specific item as the one which is taxed in the highest bracket is questionable. Moreover, in the case of loss items it is evident that the existence of a tax-saving is related not only to the loss but is also dependent on the existence of taxable income to offset the expense.

The S.E.C. illustrates another possible difficulty of the effect to be given to the carry-back, carry-forward provisions of the income tax law:

> Suppose that a loss has been charged to surplus but is deductible for taxes. Suppose further that in accordance with the present proposal there is charged to income, as provision for taxes, the amount of $200,000 although the actual tax amounts to only $50,000. If in the next year the company suffers an operating loss of $500,000, then in view of the carry-back provisions the reader of the two income statements would reasonably expect to find a carry-back refund of $200,000--the amount shown as taxes in the first year. However, obviously no more than $50,000 would actually be refundable. The question arises whether having overstated taxes in the first year it is not necessary, to be consistent, to overstate the refund in the second year. Finally, there are the permutations in the computation where a company pays taxes as a member of a consolidated group. In addition to the allocation of the actual tax paid among the several companies in the group, the proposed treatment raises the difficult question of whether the amount of so-called "saving" is to be computed on the basis of a company's individual status or on that of the consolidated group and once this is

---

[1] Committee on Accounting Procedure, op. cit., p. 39, has the following comments on the computation of tax effects: "In most cases, it is appropriate to consider the tax effect as the difference between the tax payable with and without including the item in the amount of taxable income."

decided, of whether to allocate this "saving" as between the several companies or attribute it solely to the company having the deduction--even though perhaps it itself contributed no taxable income.[1]

Another question is the wisdom of isolating income taxes for an adjustment because it does not have a "normal" relationship to reported taxable income. The "normal" relationships of most revenue and expense items are often difficult to appraise. For example, in times of recession, selling costs may be very high because of additional sales effort necessary to maintain volume, or very low because of forced cutbacks due to decreasing volume, the closing of branches, or the dropping of some lines of product. Repairs may be unusually high because of the struggle to keep going with available plant and machines or unusually low because of dampened production volume or severe cutbacks in operating expenses of all kinds. Thus since many categories of expense and revenue are likely to be abnormal as years pass, there appears to be minor justification for isolating income taxes for normalizing.

Another difficulty in this area has statistical implications. The Institute method permits accountants to show taxes in the income statement at more than taxes paid or payable for the year. In the preparation of general statistical data from financial reports, such items are totaled for a period of years and for industry groups. Aggregates could be compiled which would be erroneous representations of the underlying facts.

Essentially the basis for rejecting the normalizing and pro-rating of income taxes rests upon the contention that the

---

[1]Securities and Exchange Commission, Accounting Series Releases, op. cit., p. 154.

income statement should attempt to reveal as clearly as possible the actual happenings of the year. The statement should not undertake to present "if" happenings in regard to income taxes. The statement should undertake the presentation of financial <u>history</u> so that it can be readily analyzed. Accountancy should not usurp one of the functions of the financial analyst by "normalizing," a process leading to gross misrepresentation and misinterpretation at worst and leading to a meaningless, single figure summary at best. This position will be elaborated in the following section.

Conclusions

As has been mentioned previously, both the attempts of the Institute to develop criteria for drawing a sharp net income result, one that best reflects "normal" earning power, and the Association's and S.E.C.'s support of the all-inclusive approach point toward the inherent weaknesses in the determination of a net income figure.

The Institute's attempts are in harmony with the analysts' expressed desires for a "normal" net income figure. But the Association and the S.E.C. have serious doubts about the practical results of such an approach. It seems that the reasonable implications for accountants of the above issues are as outlined in the following paragraphs.

Accountants generally agree that financial statements are historical in nature. Attempts are made to account for revenues which have actually been earned. The balance sheet attempts to show those costs that are of benefit to future operations. The earnings statement involves the problem of determining what portion of costs actually incurred should be released as expenses or losses, and what portion of the asset inflows may be recognized as revenues. The matching of revenues and expenses yields a difference called income or earnings.

Thus financial accounting deals with what did happen, not with what might happen if conditions had been different. The financial statements do not try to forecast the future even though they furnish many of the tools used in making such a forecast.

Efforts should be made to present the results of operations in a format which is as helpful as possible for the purpose of aiding judgments as to future prospects. In general, non-recurring items are set apart and clearly distinguished so that the reader is aware of them. Then he can decide whether such items can be expected to reappear.

The "normal" income adherents feel that a sharp income is more reliable for estimating the future because the statement better indicates what can happen year after year. A major justification for such an approach is that if the actual results are unusual, a reader may be misled into thinking the abnormalities will recur. There are several limitations inherent in the "normal" net income notion. First, the accountant's and/or manager's judgments as to what is abnormal can hardly be deemed infallible. Second, there is as strong a likelihood that the statement reader will fail to understand what has been done in "normalizing" as there is that he will fail to recognize that the all-inclusive figure is abnormal. Third, and most important, the sharp net income approach is "extremely susceptible of misuse through conscious or unconscious bias in making decisions as to what is unusual or abnormal about the current year."[1]

Considering the contrasting opinions it would seem a judicious move on the part of accountants to abandon the search for a definition of "net income" which can possibly satisfy all interested parties. Fundamentally, net income, especially for one year, is a tenuous and subjective notion. The variety of accounting procedures applied by enterprises in the measurement of "net income" raises serious questions as to the usefulness of comparing the net incomes of similar firms. Moreover, comparisons of annual fluctuations in income of a single firm requires careful examination of changes in the major factors which determine the figure.

Progress in recent years on the part of accounting bodies and writers toward lessening the widespread confusion concerning the meaning and uses of "reserves" has been encouraging. This progress has been high-lighted by the trend toward abandoning the term "reserve." It is conceivable that accounting bodies might help lessen the universal confusion concerning the meaning of "net income" by rejecting the term altogether.[2] However, this writer's suggestions are being made against the backdrop of the entity theory, because that is the basis usually employed in the thinking of accountants and in applications of accounting methods to profit-seeking enterprises.

---

[1]Securities and Exchange Commission, Accounting Series Releases, p. 146.

[2]Vatter, op. cit.

The above analysis leads this writer to conclude that the most useful function of the statement of operations is to present an accurate historical summary. If the Institute's and analysts' position favoring a sharp figure were widely adopted, the dangers of overemphasizing the net income figure would be accentuated. The illusion of precision would be amplified rather than mitigated.

Greer and Wilcox pointed toward the dangers of the sharp income approach as follows:

> The approach to income determination as an indication of earning power is fraught with dangers which must not be forgotten in a fine flush of overenthusiasm. Since earning power is only significant with respect to the future, it would be logical to conclude that income statements reflecting earning power should be pro-forma rather than historical in any sense. Such statements could then be prepared as frank estimates of future earnings. Assumptions underlying them would include estimates of future market and price trends, efficiencies to be attained, expansion, and so forth. To the extent that such assumptions were good guesses, the representations in such statements would indicate the prospects of future income.
>
> But pro-forma statements and income reporting are not synonymous, and the danger of confusion between them is serious. It is for this reason that paragraph (12) of the rules of professional conduct of the American Institute of Accountants forbids the use of a member's name in conjunction with future estimates in a manner which may lead to the belief that he vouches for their accuracy. Experience has taught us that he cannot substitute pro-forma for historical statements. Admittedly there is no clear line between them, but pro-forma statements necessarily embody "as-if" assumptions, *and an adjustment of costs as if they had been incurred today is basically pro-forma in nature. But this single concession to pro-forma concepts, without other related concessions, will produce a statement which is neither one thing nor the other, but a misleading nonentity of greatly impaired significance with respect to earning power.*[1]

The items included in an income statement should clearly

---

[1] H.C. Greer and E.B. Wilcox, "The Case Against Price Level Adjustments in Income Determination," *Journal of Accountancy*, XCIV, No. 5 (November, 1952), 569. (My italics)

and concisely reflect what has happened. Accordingly, the items should not be adjusted to reflect amounts that the accountant or manager consider to be more "normal" or likely to recur in future years. It is not the task of the accountant to adjust items so as to eliminate the effect of unusual circumstances which actually occurred.[1]

For example, the sale of corporate property at a material loss is an important fact. It is no less important because such an event occurs in a year of high tax rates and high income so as to effect a substantial reduction in income taxes payable. In such a case there are two facts to be revealed--the loss on the property, and its tax ramifications. Such a transaction ought to be reported without concealing either the fact that a loss was suffered or the amount of the loss.[2] To report this kind of

---

[1]Maurice E. Peloubet, "Advantages of the Historical Income Statement," in Termination and Taxes (New York: American Institute of Accountants, 1944), p. 189, makes the following comments with respect to normalizing income statements: "For all these reasons, the attempt to prepare an account for a definite period of time in which one group of figures are in effect labeled, 'Figures to be taken into consideration in determining future earnings' and another group labeled, 'Figures which have no significance or relation to future earnings,' is bound to be misleading. As I have tried to show, we cannot take a short period in the life of a business and describe exactly what happens within that period, no more, no less. If we cannot do that, then we cannot always distinguish between items which definitely and certainly apply to transactions prior to the period. We can and should indicate what items occur in the normal course of business and what are extraordinary and unusual, but it seems to me improper and misleading to attempt to separate these extraordinary and unusual items into those which refer to the past, as distinguished from those which should affect the current period's operations."

[2]The reporting of the sale in 1953 of Fieldcrest Mills by Marshall Field and Company is an example in this respect. The only reference to the sale is found in the statement of Earned Surplus as "Net credit . . . including related tax reductions . . . . $577,538." The explanation in the president's letter is far from illuminating. Marshall Field and Co., Annual Report, 1953.

loss net of tax consequences is no more justifiable than to report on a similar net basis an expense such as salaries, depreciation or insurance.

Keeping in mind the above comments, the following specific suggestions as to reporting practice are recommended as being the most informative, the least misleading, and the most useful:

Report of Operations and Reconciliation of Retained Earnings

Sales.	$xxx
Less: Operating Expenses.	xxx
Operating Margin	$xxx
Add (deduct): Non-recurring items	xxx[a]
Net Margin before Income Taxes	$xxx
Provision for Income Taxes	.xxx[b]
All-inclusive Margin (or over-all earnings, final earnings, all-inclusive earnings, net margin)	$xxx
Add: Retained Earnings, balance at beginning of year	xxx
Total.	$xxx
Deduct: Dividends	xxx
Ending balance, Retained Earnings.	$xxx

[a]Material non-recurring items (a) should be itemized individually; (b) should not offset one another nor be offset by income tax allocations; and (c) should be accompanied by thorough footnote explanations of the transactions involved, including the amount and basis for determination of gains or losses.

[b]The amount of income taxes payable for the current year, accompanied by a footnote or supplementary schedule explaining details whenever the amount is substantially different from the amount which would be calculated by applying current rates.

The above presentation has the following features:

1. The separate "income statement" and the term "net income" would be abandoned completely. Instead the statement could be referred to perhaps as a "Report of Operations and Reconciliation of Retained Earnings." The current trend toward combining the statements is a desirable one which deserves more prodding

than the "it-would-be-nice-if-you-did-it-but-you-don't-have-to" attitude of the American Institute of Accountants.[1] The concentration on a single net income figure would be properly deemphasized.

2. Instead of prolonging the squabbling over what "net income" should be, this statement offers the following attractions: The operating margin is clearly drawn, but it is followed by non-recurring items and actual income tax charges which lead to the final impact (before dividends) of the firm's transactions on retained earnings. This final impact is referred to descriptively as "all-inclusive margin" or "all-inclusive earnings." If the adjective "all-inclusive" were adopted and quoted by newspapers and statistical services, there should be little doubt in the readers' minds as to what was implied. Of course, pleas for the quoting of two figures ("normal" and "all-inclusive" net income figures) are the most feasible answer to the problem.[2]

3. The sharp net income proponents would be satisfied to the degree that the operating margin is distinctly drawn, and to the degree that current income tax rates may be applied to the margin if the reader so desires.

4. Footnotes should be made more revealing and more specific in explaining the significance and nature of extraordinary items. A thoroughgoing explanation should include the basis for determining gain or loss, the proceeds, and, only if capital gains taxes are involved, the amount of the income tax effects.

---

[1]Committee on Accounting Procedure, op. cit., pp. 17-18.

[2]Maurice Stans, "Modernizing the Income Statement," Accounting Review, XXIV, No. 1 (January, 1949), p. 6.

Last, attention should be centered upon the problem of relating the preparation of financial statements to their purpose. The ultimate purpose of financial statements is to strive toward maximum utility for the reader. From the analyst's vantage point the zenith of maximum utility probably would be a neat figure portraying <u>future</u> earnings per share drawn by a clairvoyant individual. But are steps in this direction within the province of the accountant?[1] What is a statement of operations, anyway? It is a statement which should convey a reasonably detailed, complete, clear story of the financial impact of transactions upon the firm. The future lies <u>ahead</u>; elements of possible forthcoming events do not belong in the body of a financial statement. The accountant's products should supply the analyst with a well-told story of the past accompanied by ample information (not in the body of the statement) concerning management's misgivings or hopes for the future. But the accountant is not and should not become a financial analyst. It is the analyst's task to determine "normal" or prospective earnings. Certainly the analyst should not be handicapped in his efforts by misleading or sketchy statements. That is why further disclosure and amplified descriptions are the most pressing problems of financial reporting today. This writer believes that the suggested format for a "Statement of Operations and Reconciliation of Retained

---

[1]Peloubet, <u>op. cit</u>., p. 151, commented: "The best we can say for accounts of the past as guides to future is that when they are carefully prepared and properly adjusted, to show as nearly as possible the actual results of operations, we can then apply various tests and assumptions to them which may produce a reliable guide to the future. The attempt to do this through ordinary accounting processes only is dangerous, misleading and bound to fail."

Earnings" is superior to any efforts toward drafting a "sharp" statement leading to a figure labeled "net income," with its fictitious stamp of indelible finality.

CHAPTER VII

THE ANALYST'S USE OF FIXED ASSET DATA

This chapter is (a) an attempt to outline the demands of analysts for certain types of information as reflected by their uses of fixed asset data in their analyses, and (b) an attempt to focus upon the areas where immediate improvements in fixed asset reporting may be made.

As will be indicated in the passages from written financial analyses which follow, money spent on plant and equipment and the source of such money overshadow the book values of fixed assets both in importance and in usefulness. The following factors appear to be the most significant in the analysis of fixed assets.

1. Emphasis on Future

Analysts attempt to estimate the increments in future sales and in profits which probably will flow from current and planned expansion.[1] Their estimates are usually based upon

---

[1]Jeremy C. Jenks, "Projecting Corporate Earnings," The Analysts Journal, IX, No. 1 (February, 1953), 101, states: "From the projected figures on gross plant it is possible to jump directly to a projection of normal earnings after taxes. Managements watch the figure of return on investment very carefully. For that matter, it appears that return on investment is the most important determinant of whether or not a new plant expansion program will be undertaken in the chemical industry. Each company has its own method of determining what is included in investment. In most cases companies take gross plant, not net

information obtained from direct contacts with company officials or upon an analysis of past relationships between capital spending and sales or profit increases. For instance, in the cases of Union Carbide and Dow Chemical in recent years a dollar spent on plant has been followed by a dollar increase in sales.[1] Of course, these are rule-of-thumb procedures; they are modified according to the specific situation.

The probable impact of capital expenditures on financial position, earnings, and dividends are invariably discussed by analysts in their written reports. The following excerpt from an analysis of National Lead illustrates the type of estimates involved:

> It is estimated that National Lead accounted for 48.5 per cent (170,000 tons) of total 1951 production of titanium dioxide. The remainder was divided among du Pont (28.5 per cent) American Cyanamid (14.4 per cent) and Glidden (8.6 per cent). National Lead's recently completed $20 million additional productive capacity will raise its total production to 250,000 tons annually and will further broaden its leadership in the field. Assuming capacity operations and continuation of the current price of 23 1/2 cents per pound, the increased production could add some $20 million, or about 5 per cent, to sales. Pretax margins are much wider than for other lines, possibly running as high as 30 per cent. This would add $6.0 million to pretax profits but since the company

---

plant, and add to it an amount that represents working capital requirements and other items. For the purposes of security analysts it is usually sufficient to relate earnings to gross plant by itself. The figures differ somewhat, depending on how they are worked out, but earnings for well-managed chemical companies seem to average over 10 per cent on gross plant, which is usually taken at the beginning of the year.

"Earnings related to investment vary from year to year for reasons other than the rate of business activity or taxes. For example, a large part of Dow's expansion has gone into capacity for basic chemicals. . . . The net return on this type of plant facility is lower than normal, perhaps averaging 9 per cent after taxes at a 60 per cent level. . . . Over the next several years, the character of Dow's plant expansion program is going to shift . . . where the return on investment will be a great deal higher, estimated at about 12 to 15 per cent after a 60 per cent tax."

[1] *Ibid.*, p. 101.

> is already subject to EPT liability, 82 per cent will go for taxes. Thus tax relief will be necessary before this increase will add materially to net.

Obviously, knowledge of the types of new products or processes which will develop out of capital expansion or capital replacement is of extreme significance.

2. Operating Policies

Also of paramount importance in the emphasis upon capital expenditures is that such spending is one of the better indicators of operating policies. Analysts are keenly interested in the ability of a company to maintain and enhance its competitive position; and capital spending is regarded as one of the best reflections of the intentions of management toward product development, product diversification, process improvement, and cost control. In this regard the wisdom of the management is judged by its recent (past five to seven years) performance with capital expenditures. Such recent performance is evidenced primarily by the relationship of sales, earnings, and dividends to capital outlays.

The following excerpt from an analysis of the Hazel-Atlas Glass Company illustrates analysts' feelings toward managements' capital expansion plans:

> 5. New developments--Expansion Program: Last year the company announced plans for an expansion program which included the construction of a new plant in the Chicago area and one in New Jersey. A plant site was acquired at Plainfield, Illinois, but no construction has taken place to date.
>
> Mr. McNash, President of Hazel-Atlas, talking with our representative, explained the company's philosophy concerning the expansion program. The program would eventually involve a plant containing two glass furnaces and a warehouse at Plainfield, a two-furnace plant in New Jersey, and the addition of a furnace to the Montgomery, Alabama plant.

The total program would add a maximum of five furnaces to the thirty now in operation and, therefore, would be a relatively modest expansion program. Mr. McNash stated that the company expects to earn about 10 per cent after taxes on the new units, or about what the company currently earns on its net worth. The ability to earn this rate of return on the new plant, whose cost would be much higher than the book value of the existing plant, is predicated on savings in freight costs rather than on improvement in operating efficiency, according to Mr. McNash.

There is, however, some doubt that savings in freight costs alone would permit the company to earn as much as 10 per cent after taxes on additional capital assuming that both old and new capacity were fully utilized. Given the slow prospective growth in demand for glass containers additional doubt is generated concerning the prospect that new plant would make a generous contribution in the near future. Accordingly, our representative raised a question as to the wisdom of expanding productive capacity at this time. In answer, Mr. McNash stressed again the necessity of overcoming the handicap of high freight costs as well as the need to improve delivery service to customers located at long distances from existing plants. Thus, competitive factors, rather than the expectation of substantial return on additional invested capital, seem to be decisive in the company's thoughts about expansion.

The company has held up action on the expansion program because of high building costs. Mr. McNash stated that last year bids received on the projected plant and warehouse at Plainfield totaled $8.5 million. This was much higher than the company's estimates and the bids were rejected. Mr. McNash believes that the high bids were accounted for by lack of interest in the job at that time on the part of the contractors. A recent bid for the two furnace plants and warehouse received by Hazel-Atlas was $5.5 million. This is about what the company thinks the installation should cost and a decision on whether or not to accept it will be made early next year. With the possible exception of the additional furnace proposed for the Montgomery, Alabama, plant, near term action on the expansion program would probably include only the Plainfield plant. The $8 million currently held by the company in Government securities should be ample to cover the cost of this project.

In the meantime, to improve delivery service to customers, warehouse space has been rented at Rockdale, Illinois, Kearney, New Jersey, and Chester, Pennsylvania. The Rockdale warehouse, for example, has 65,000 square feet and truck deliveries are made from it to customers in the Chicago and northern Illinois area. Warehouse space is being added to the Montgomery, Alabama, and Oakland, California, plants also. . . .

10. Long Range Valuation: In discussing the long range objectives of Hazel-Atlas with Mr. McNash, our representative asked if the company intended to make a concerted effort to shift its product mix in favor of wider profit margin, machine-made glassware. Mr. McNash stated that *if* a plant were

built at Plainfield perhaps more of the company's capacity could be devoted to production of these items. Asked whether Hazel-Atlas would consider entering the polyethylene field as has Owens-Illinois, Mr. McNash stated that he was not too seriously worried about the competition of polyethylene with glass for containers and indicated that the company would not be interested in entering this field. Furthermore, he stressed the fact that Owens-Illinois has a great deal more capital than Hazel-Atlas and could afford to risk money in new enterprises whereas his company has enough projects in its glass business to make use of the capital it has available.

The discussion above is presented as illustrative of management philosophy concerning future operations of the company. It tends to indicate a continuation of the rather acute conservatism which has held development of Hazel-Atlas behind that of other industry leaders. As has been noted previously, the expansion program, as currently envisioned by management, is not liable to add much to earning power for some time. Certainly caution is well advised in managing a company in the competitive glass container industry, but it would seem that unless the company can find ways to increase the proportion of sales in lines which return a higher profit than the wide-neck food container, its status in the industry will continue to decline.

3. Financial Policies

Obviously company financial policies are intertwined with management's plans for capital expenditures. The source of the funds is of prime interest. Furthermore, the decisions as to what to do with available funds offer concrete portrayals of managerial thinking.

For instance, most analysts take a favorable view of the tendency in retailing for firms to adopt long-term lease arrangements for facilities rather than to assume outright ownership. Analysts have concluded that retailers can secure larger returns from capital invested in retailing operations rather than in real estate and equipment.[1] The following excerpts from an analysis of Marshall Field reflect this attitude:

---

[1] Also see section, "Long-term Leases" (*infra*).

> The extremely low sales to net property ratio for Field combined with its comparatively low return on net worth figure and low rent to sales ratio are enlightening. These figures indicate that Field has a much higher proportion of its capital invested in real estate than the other companies and suggest that retail operations currently provide a higher rate of return than do funds invested in department store real estate. . . .
>
> Thus it seems that common stockholders may benefit either from sale and leaseback of store properties (as in the case of Federated and May) or heavier financing of real estate by debt rather than equity funds (as in the case of Allied). It appears that the Field management has recognized the relative unprofitability of owning store real estate as it plans to lease all three of the planned new stores.

Analysts invariably scrutinize the impact of capital outlays upon the working capital position. Since recent external financing has been largely in the form of debt, analysts always estimate and relate debt service outlays to projected earnings. When funds for financing have been generated internally, analysts are vitally concerned with prospective effects upon dividend policy. Obviously, if management has adopted the policy of internal financing, the dividend pay-outs in relation to earnings tend to suffer.

The points in the preceding paragraph are illustrated by the following analyst's appraisal of Chrysler's current situation:

> Expenditures for engineering and tooling of the new Chrysler Corporation models are no doubt requiring substantial and increasing amounts of working capital. The tooling for its 1955 models is expected to cost $100-125 million plus $25 million or more related expenses. Competition will probably require Chrysler's spending considerably more on its model changes than in the past and such sums will "tie up" $100 million of its working capital--or roughly $50 million more than the annual average tooling investment in 1952 and 1953.
>
> . . . an important part of the new money will be required to build up Chrysler's working capital position. Its present $199 million working capital (before any proceeds from the loan) compares with $195 million at the end of World War II and with a high of $340 million in 1949. Perhaps $300-350

> million would be a reasonable working capital figure for Chrysler to reflect inflation and its postwar volume level.
> . . . conclude in regard to Chrysler's recent plans to borrow $250 million that the full amount will meet only its minimum requirements for additional funds over the next two or three years. A corollary of this seems to be a conservative dividend policy.

The importance of disclosure of the details of the working capital position in relation to budgeted capital expenditures is pointed out in the recommendations of the National Federation of Financial Analysts Societies with respect to the annual reports of the oil companies:

> . . . the principal observations and recommendations are as follows. . . .
> 2. Discuss frankly the working capital position in relation to budgeted capital expenditures, particularly where there are prospects of new financing. Of the three major new financings undertaken in the past year by Socony Vacuum, Standard Oil of Indiana, and Sinclair, none made any mention in its 1951 report of the possibility that new financing was contemplated. Standard Oil of Indiana's report implied that no financing was anticipated.[1]

Accelerated Depreciation

One of the major problems faced by the user of financial statements is the one posed by depreciation. Accounting literature is sprinkled with remarks such as the following: "Depreciation accounting is a system of accounting which aims to distribute the cost or other basic value of tangible capital assets, less salvage (if any), over the estimated useful life of the unit in a systematic and rational manner. It is a process of allocation, not of valuation."[2] Judgment as to "useful life" is a difficult

---

[1]Committee on Corporate Information, National Federation of Financial Analyst Societies, Reports of National Committees for 1953 (New York: New York Society of Security Analysts, Inc., 1954), p. 15.

[2]Committee on Terminology, American Institute of Accountants, Accounting Terminology Bulletins, No. 1, Review and Resume (New York: American Institute of Accountants, 1953), p. 25.

task, and depreciation methods often vary markedly between companies within the same industry.[1] In durable goods industries depreciation is often a leading component of the expenses matched against revenue in determining net income. Consequently, the comparisons of similar heavy goods companies often require close examination of depreciation methods.

The income tax law can be both blessed and damned for its contribution to depreciation accounting. It can be blessed because depreciation has become recognized by businessmen as an expense. Before the law was enacted many executives ignored the idea that depreciation is a component of the costs allocable to a given year.[2] The law can also be blessed because it instilled some uniformity into the treatment of depreciation rates for various types of fixed assets.[3] But it can be damned from a financial accounting standpoint because the law has provided for the issuance of certificates of necessity under which all or part of the cost of so-called emergency facilities may be amortized over a period of sixty months for income-tax purposes.[4] Thus many firms are faced with the decision of adopting the sixty month period or of adopting a strict "useful life" basis for financial reporting purposes, even though the sixty month basis is used for tax purposes.

---

[1]Chemical, Aluminum and Petroleum industries offer examples of widely varying depreciation and amortization policies.

[2]H.A. Finney and H.E. Miller, Principles of Accounting--Intermediate (4th ed.; New York: Prentice-Hall, Inc., 1951), p. 438.

[3]U.S. Treasury Department--Bureau of Internal Revenue, Bulletin "F" Income Tax Depreciation and Obsolesence Estimated Useful Lives and Depreciation Rates (Washington, D.C.: U.S. Government Printing Office, 1948).

[4]U.S. Treasury Department--Bureau of Internal Revenue, Revenue Act of 1950 (Washington, D.C.: U.S. Government Printing Office, 1950), Section 124 A.

Current Accounting Practice

The American Institute of Accountants feels that proper reporting requires the adoption of a "useful life" basis for the allocation of depreciation charges. The Institute's position in the matter of certificates of necessity is presented as follows:

> . . . is of the opinion that from an accounting standpoint there is nothing inherent in the nature of emergency facilities which requires the depreciation or amortization of their cost for financial accounting purposes over either a shorter or a longer period than would be proper if no certificate of necessity had been issued. Estimates of the probable useful life of a facility by those best informed in the matter may indicate either a shorter or a longer life than the statutory 60 month period over which the certified portion of its cost is deductible for income-tax purposes.[1]

In discussing depreciation for accounting purposes, the committee states that it

> . . . believes that when the amount allowed as amortization for income-tax purposes is materially different from the amount of the estimated depreciation, the latter should be used for financial accounting purposes.[2]

The committee also relates the above treatment to the reporting of income taxes by advocating the adjusting and deferring of income tax charges in accordance with what taxes "would have been" if accelerated amortization had not been taken.[3]

---

[1] Committee on Accounting Procedure, American Institute of Accountants, Accounting Research Bulletin No. 43: Restatement and Revision of Accounting Research Bulletins (New York: The American Institute of Accountants, 1953), pp. 76-77.

[2] Ibid., p. 77.

[3] Ibid., pp. 78-79. The Committee states: "In those cases in which the amount of depreciation charged in the accounts on that portion of the cost of the facilities for which certificates of necessity have been obtained is materially less than the amount of amortization deducted for income-tax purposes, the amount of income taxes payable annually during the amortization period may be significantly less than it would be on the basis of the income reflected in the financial statements. In such cases, after the

Out of 600 annual reports for 1952, 170 referred to approved certificates of necessity. There were 124 instances disclosed where amortization under certificates of necessity was being taken for both book and tax purposes, and eleven instances where such amortization was being claimed for tax purposes only.[1]

The following table summarizes the current accounting treatment and presentation of amortization under certificates of necessity.

Clearly, the overwhelming majority of firms armed with certificates of necessity have chosen the sixty-month period for financial reporting purposes. It is also noteworthy that over 50

---

close of the amortization period the income taxes will exceed the amount that would be appropriate on the basis of the income reported in the statements. Accordingly, the committee believes that during the amortization period, where this difference is material, a charge should be made in the income statement to recognize the income tax to be paid in the future on the amount by which amortization for income-tax purposes exceeds the depreciation that would be allowable if certificates of necessity had not been issued. The amount of the charge should be equal to the estimated amount by which the income tax expected to be payable after the amortization period exceeds what would be so expected if amortization had not been claimed for income-tax purposes in the amortization period. The estimated amount should be based upon normal and surtax rates in effect during the period covered by the income statement with such changes therein as can be reasonably anticipated at the time the estimate is made.

In accounting for the deferment of income taxes, the committee believes it desirable to treat the charge as being for additional income taxes. The related credit in such cases would properly be made to an account for deferred income taxes. Under this method, during the life of the facility following the amortization period the annual charges for income taxes will be reduced by charging to the account for deferred income taxes that part of the income tax in excess of what would have been payable had the amortization deduction not been claimed for income-tax purposes in the amortization period. By this procedure the net income will more nearly reflect the results of a proper matching of costs and revenues."

[1]Research Department of the American Institute of Accountants, Accounting Trends and Techniques, 1953 edition (New York: American Institute of Accountants, 1953), p. 190.

TABLE 9

ACCELERATED AMORTIZATION UNDER CERTIFICATES OF NECESSITY

	1952	1951
For both book and tax purposes:		
Charge for accelerated amortization separately set forth in:		
Statement of income	24	15
Notes to financial statements	28	25
Letter to stockholders.	18	7
Charge for accelerated amortization combined with normal depreciation set forth in:		
Statement of income	5	6
Notes to financial statements	21	8
Letter to stockholders.	16	5
Balance sheet or fixed asset schedule as "accumulated amortization"	12	6
Total.	124	72
For tax purpose only:		
Accelerated Amortization:		
Notes to financial statements	..	3
Accelerated amortization with charge for deferral of tax benefit attributable to certificates of necessity set forth in:		
Statement of income	6	1
Notes to financial statements	5	..
	11	4
Number of companies		
Referring to approved certificates of necessity	170	159
Referring to applications for certificates of necessity	1	14
Not referring to certificates of necessity. . .	429	437
	600	600

Source: Research Department of the American Institute of Accountants, Accounting Trends and Techniques, 1953 edition (New York: American Institute of Accountants, 1953), p. 190.

per cent of the firms adopting this method have failed to differentiate between accelerated amortization and their normal depreciation.

The 1952 annual reports of Food Machinery and Chemical Corporation, and Trans World Airlines, Inc., are examples of companies that in their accounts have charged only normal depreciation with respect to emergency facilities. In their tax returns these companies have elected to deduct accelerated amortization over the sixty-month period. They have provided a reserve in their balance sheets for deferred income taxes.

In a note to its 1952 balance sheet, The Yale and Towne Manufacturing Company sets forth supplementary information, including the amount of accelerated amortization over normal depreciation as follows:

Balance Sheet

Property, plant and equipment (Note 7). . . .	$	645,049
Land.		8,328,473
Buildings		23,799,294
Machinery and equipment		..
Property, plant and equipment (at cost) . . .		32,772,816
Less accumulated depreciation and amortization		13,201,165
Total property, plant and equipment..	$	19,571,651

Note 7: Certificates of Necessity. To December 31, 1952, facilities of an estimated cost of $2,711,781 have been approved for accelerated amortization ($2,543,274 to the extent of 60 per cent, $140,532 to the extent of 70 per cent, and $27,975 to the extent of 75 per cent), of which, facilities costing $1,655,282 have been acquired. The amortization of these facilities in excess of normal depreciation amounted to $75,351 in 1952 and $3,636 in 1951. The company has applied for approval on additional facilities to cost approximately $1,917,508.[1]

The Yale and Towne example indicates the type of disclosure which analysts desire with respect to accelerated amortization.

The conclusion which can be drawn from current practice

---

[1]The Yale and Towne Manufacturing Company, Annual Report, 1952, pp. 11, 13.

is self-evident. Generally accepted accounting principles simply are not being followed. The original costs of fixed assets should be allocated to operations on the basis of their estimated useful life. But five-year write-offs are being applied probably for two reasons: (a) to dampen reported income because of managerial desire to do so and (b) to keep reported income reasonably in line with income tax returns. Nevertheless auditing firms cling to their stereotyped phrases and approve statements which in cases of material five-year write-offs might easily be misleading.[1] The implications are obvious. Public accounting firms should take a firmer stand toward the five-year write-off plans and be certain that emergency facilities are written off in a more rational manner.[2] But it is obvious, too, that this is the ivory-tower goal. Practically speaking, the answer again centers around disclosure. Minimum disclosure requirements should include: (a) the estimated useful lives of emergency facilities, (b) the total amount of excess amortization, and (c) the differences between total depreciation charges and normal depreciation charges for each major class of emergency facilities. If the analysts are furnished with these minimum data, they should be able to apply such information to the specific comparative problem at hand.

---

[1]Nearly every auditor's letter contains an approval of the accompanying financial statements and points out that they have been prepared "in conformity with generally accepted accounting principles."

[2]It is noteworthy that public accounting firms in many cases have not hesitated to overlook companies' questionable accounting treatments and scanty disclosures in cases of emergency facilities.

The Analyst's Viewpoint

The Siamese problems that disturb the analyst the most about depreciation reporting are (a) the lack of information concerning over-all depreciation policy and especially breakdowns between "normal" depreciation and "abnormal" depreciation and (b) the difficulty of comparing companies within industries because of the different accounting policies and procedures employed.

Analysts commonly complain that companies neglect to divide their yearly depreciation charges. But, even if the amounts of "emergency" facility costs charged to operations are revealed in regard to the five-year write-offs, the analyst still must speculate as to what part of such an amount is "normal." That is, are the useful lives of "emergency" facilities seven years, ten years, twenty years, or fifty years?

Corliss Anderson, a Chicago analyst, reflected the uniform opinion of the financial community when he said: "The accounting fraternity has a real obligation to disclose the details of depreciation charges. Especially important is a breakdown between normal depreciation amounts and excess depreciation charged because of fast five-year write-offs supported by certificates of necessity."[1]

A spokesman for the Committee on Corporate Information of the National Federation of Financial Analysts Societies wrote: "Another bothersome variation is in the handling of accelerated amortization. Disclosure of the amount of such amortization and the tax savings resulting therefrom, as well as the method of

---

[1]Corliss Anderson of the firm of Duff, Anderson and Clark, personal interview, Chicago, Illinois, April 13, 1954.

handling both, should be made."[1]

The difficulty of comparing companies within industries is reflected by the following excerpt from the Committee on Corporate Information's proposals for improvements of oil companies' annual reports:

> . . . the principal observations and recommendations are as follows:
>
> 1. A more uniform system be adopted for reporting annual charges for depreciation, depletion, retirements, and exploration. Seldom do two companies report these items similarly. The result is that, when attempting to compare cash income or gross operating profits of two or more companies, it is often impossible to obtain comparable figures.
> It is recommended strongly that as a minimum the following three items be shown separately in the income statement:
> (a) Exploratory costs--including geophysical and geological expenses, dry hole costs. . . .
> (b) Amortization of intangible drilling costs.
> (c) Depreciation and depletion..
> In a footnote, account for differences between the above items and those taken for tax purposes.[2]

An analysts subcommittee on aircraft industry annual reporting included the following among its recommendations:

> . . . the following data would be useful. . . .
> . . . an analysis of the plant account indicating dollar investment in plant subject to normal depreciation and that subject to rapid amortization indicating the amount of accelerated amortization, if any, charged to the year's operation.[3]

The following excerpt from a written analysis of The Aluminum Company of America (Alcoa) exemplifies the type of

---

[1]E. Linwood Savage, Jr., "Conclusions Regarding Annual Reports," The Analysts Journal, X, No. 1 (February, 1954), 31.

[2]Committee on Corporate Information, op. cit., p. 15.

[3]Sub Committee on Aircraft Industry Annual Reporting, "Aircraft Industry Annual Reporting--1953," a mimeographed report for private distribution, April 7, 1954, p. 3. Similar comments were also found in unpublished reports of Sub Committees on annual reports of the Drug Companies, the Chemical Companies, and the Paper Companies.

thinking which analysts apply to the problems of accelerated amortization:

> Earnings were $4.71 per share. This was after excess profits taxes of $0.83 a share and accelerated amortization charges of $3.38 (before taxes) per share. In the absence of the special amortization charges and assuming a tax rate of 46 per cent (Alcoa's normal and surtax rate last year) the company apparently would have earned between $6.80 and $7.00 per share. Earnings through 1959 will be subject to heavy amortization charges reaching a peak of about $5.00 per share (pretax) in 1955. Thus reported earnings during this period will not be a true representation of the company's earning power. As to 1954, we would expect earnings to exceed last year's $4.71 per share, although rapid amortization charges will increase to about $4.65 per share (pretax).

Many analysts tend to use a "cash earnings" basis rather than a "reported earnings" basis in the valuation of stocks in the petroleum, chemical, and aluminum industries. This approach has been adopted because of the widespread variations in depreciation policies plus the difficulty of comparing similar firms which have invested in a large proportion of fixed assets at different price levels. For example, Dow Chemical Company has mushroomed in capacity since the war. Its investment in plant and equipment was largely made in the postwar years, whereas Union Carbide and du Pont had made substantial investments prior to 1941.

The following passage from the Alcoa analysis illustrates the problems of comparison in these types of industries:

> The market appears to be valuing all of the aluminum producers' stocks on the basis of cash earnings rather than on reported earnings. All are selling at a high price times reported earnings except for Reynolds which reports its earnings on a different basis from the other companies with respect to accelerated amortization and income taxes. It has adopted the policy recommended by the American Institute of Accountants which has the effect of overstating current earnings as compared to those of the other aluminum producers. . . .
>
> On a cash earnings basis, Alcoa and Aluminum, Ltd., at 7.0xand 6.7x, respectively, command a much higher ratio than either of the other producers, reflecting their favored position in the industry. It is interesting to note that

> Kaiser's cash earnings are believed to be about the same as those of Alcoa (around $11.00 per share) yet Alcoa at 75 is almost two and one-half times Kaiser's current market price of 32.

Long-term Leases

One of the salient shortcomings of present-day financial reporting is the scanty information concerning long-term lease arrangements. Every analyst who is concerned with industries where long-term leases are significant expressed his dissatisfaction with corporate information in this respect.[1]

The position of the analysts is well summarized in the following statement by E. Linwood Savage, Jr.:

> Another piece of information not usually available to us, unless we consult 10K reports to the SEC, is the amount of rentals paid. This may not be significant in many cases, but, where it is, it should not be necessary for us to go to the expense and inconvenience of securing the information from reports made to governmental bodies.[2]

The rash of sale and lease-back transactions which has taken place in the postwar years has forced analysts to be exceptionally careful in comparing firms in industries where such financial arrangements are widespread. The retailing industry is the primary example. Sears-Roebuck, Gimbel Bros., Allied Stores, and S.S. Kresge Company are some of the firms which have used the sale and lease-back vehicle. To raise funds for expansion, and to obtain tax advantages, many merchandising concerns sold store properties and rented them back under long-term leases,

---

[1]Committee on Corporate Information, "Fourth Annual Report," The Analysts Journal, VIII, No. 4 (August, 1952), 216, specifically recommends disclosure of "The amount of rentals paid, as shown on the annual report form 10K to the SEC."

[2]E. Linwood Savage, Jr., op. cit., p. 32.

which carried payments sufficient to amortize all or a good part of the cost to the purchaser. The result has been to create larger rentals in relation to business done; and in good part to replace the older type of bonded debt, which was visible on the balance sheet, with long-term lease obligations which are relatively invisible. The invisibility of these long-term commitments in most corporate reports (involving leases) considerably hampers the efforts of the analyst.

Of course, analysts attempt to measure the fixed charge coverage because the high level of rentals assumed in prosperous years might become overwhelmingly oppressive if earnings decline. Graham and Dodd establish the importance of this factor with the following example:

> The influence of this factor upon a supposed investment security is shown with striking force in the case of United Cigar Stores Preferred. This issue and its predecessor had for many years shown every sign of stability and had sold accordingly at a consistently high level. For 1928 the company reported "no Funded debt" and earnings equal to about seven times the preferred dividend. Yet so crushing were the liabilities under its long-term leases . . . that in 1932 bankruptcy was resorted to and the preferred stock was menaced with extinction.[1]

Both the Securities and Exchange Commission and the American Institute of Accountants have taken the stand that full disclosure should be made in the financial statements of the amounts of annual rentals to be paid under long-term leases.[2]

---

[1]B. Graham and D. Dodd, Security Analysis (3rd ed.; New York: McGraw Hill, Inc., 1951), p. 382.

[2]Securities and Exchange Commission, Regulation S-X (Washington, D.C.: U.S. Government Printing Office, 1951), Rule 3-18 (6). Committee on Accounting Procedure, American Institute of Accountants, Accounting Research Bulletin, No. 43, Restatement and Revision of Accounting Research Bulletins (New York: American Institute of Accountants, 1953), pp. 125-127.

Some indication of the periods for which rentals are payable and any other important obligation assumed or guaranteed in connection with leases should also be revealed. But, as can be seen from the paragraphs which follow, corporate reporting with respect to long-term leases is not particularly informative, to say the least.

In the American Institute survey there were 164 of the 600 survey companies that referred, in one way or another, in their 1952 reports to the existence of long-term leases. Of these, 90 firms merely mentioned or indicated that such leases existed but did not include any details thereof.[1] The remaining 74 companies in this group set forth in varying degrees such factual data as the amount of the annual rental or the aggregate rental, the term of the lease or its expiration date, the number of leases, information as to renewal options, and details as to sell-and-leaseback provisions. The extent of the information disclosed by each of the above 74 companies may be further summarized as follows:

1 company refers only to the period covered by the lease.
1 company refers only to the period covered by the lease and to the existence of sell-and-lease back arrangements.
4 companies refer only to the existence of sell-and-lease back arrangements.
14 companies disclose only the amount of the annual rental.
54 companies, in addition to disclosing the amount of the annual rental, set forth, in varying degrees certain further information with regard to their long-term leases. This group includes Consolidated Cigar Corporation; Endicott Johnson Corporation; Gimbel Brothers, Inc.; S.H. Kress and Co.; Loew's Incorporated; J.J. Newberry Co.; Regal Shoe Company; and Allied Stores Corporation.[2]

---

[1]Included in this group are such companies as The Best Foods, Inc.; Revoe and Reynolds Company, Inc.; Kellog Company; F.W. Woolworth Co.; and Frank G. Shattuck Company.

[2]Research Department, op. cit., p. 90.

The information of the type discussed above was almost always found in the footnotes to the financial statements. Table 10 summarizes the nature of the long-term leases and the method of disclosure.

TABLE 10

LONG-TERM LEASES

Disclosures by Lessees	Details Set Forth in: Foot-notes	Letter to Stock-holders	Accountants Report	1952 Total
Annual rent amount.	65	2	1	68
Aggregate rental amount	5	1	...	6
Lease expiration date	33	...	1	34
Number of leases.	28	1	...	29
Term of lease	20	1	...	21
Renewal option.	12	...	...	12
Sell-lease-back feature	12	7	...	19
Total	175*	12	2	189
Number of companies				
Setting forth details of long-term leases				74
Mentioning long-term leases but omitting details thereof.				24
Indicating long-term leases without mention thereof by reference to leaseholds or leasehold improvements . . .				66
Total.				164
Neither referring to nor indicating long-term leases. . .				436
				600

*Includes 10 notes set forth within the balance sheet or at the foot thereof.

Source: Research Department, cited in Table 9, p. 140.

A parallel might be drawn between the disclosure of interest and sinking fund requirements on funded debt and the disclosure of rental requirements on long-term leases. Few accountants or managers would attempt to withhold such elementary information as debt-service obligations, yet a good many firms continue to be needlessly stingy with similar significant data concerning long-term leases.

Summary

The significant information which analysts desire with respect to fixed assets may be summarized as follows:

1. Past (five to seven) years capital expenditures and planned capital expenditures together with descriptions of the types of assets, products, and processes involved.

2. The probable impact of capital expenditures on financial position, earnings and dividends.

3. "The insurance value--or other current value figure--of fixed assets excluding land."[1] This is a specific recommendation of the Committee on Corporate Information of the National Federation of Financial Analysts Societies. This writer inquired among analysts about the usefulness of such information. Interestingly enough, there was general indifference as to the disclosure of such information except in cases of impending mergers of industrial concerns. One analyst expressed the general attitude as follows:

> Well, I don't know what we'd do with it if we got it. I suppose there are isolated instances where insurance values might be useful, but I can't think of any offhand. After all, corporations simply don't go out and buy a whole set of new fixed assets in one year.

4. A thorough breakdown of fixed assets by classifications

---

[1]Committee on Corporate Information, <u>op. cit</u>., p. 216.

together with a short description of the depreciation accounting policies being applied.

5. Thorough disclosure with respect to accounting for emergency facilities. The minimum essentials include (a) the amount spent on emergency facilities, (b) the total amount of excess amortization charged in the income statement and (c) the estimated useful lives of the facilities, and the difference between total depreciation charges (including five-year amortization allocations) and normal depreciation charges for each major class of emergency facilities.

6. More uniformity in depreciation policies within industries.

7. Thorough disclosure of companies' obligations under long-term lease arrangements. Such disclosure would include (a) the amount of annual rentals, (b) the length of the leases and (c) any other important obligations assumed in connection with the leases.

Executives and accountants could facilitate the analyst's task by complying as completely as possible with the above requirements. Surely, the analysts' desires do not appear to be unreasonable.

CHAPTER VIII

FIXED ASSET ANALYSIS AND THE PRICE LEVEL

In recent years accounting literature has been replete with suggested modifications in accounting and financial reporting to overcome the effects of changing price levels. The tenor of most of such writings has been that "something must be done" to make accounting results more meaningful, more useful and less misleading. There have been widely varying remedies suggested, from sweeping overhauls of fundamental approaches to adamant adherence to the status quo.[1] This chapter is an attempt to

---

[1]Cf. H.W. Sweeney, Stabilized Accounting (New York: Harper and Bros., 1936). Study Group on Business Income, Changing Concepts of Business Income (New York: Macmillan Co., 1952). S.S. Alexander et al., Five Monographs on Business Income (New York: American Institute of Accountants, 1950). George O. May, Business Income and Price Levels--An Accounting Study (New York: American Institute of Accountants, 1949). A.H. Dean, An Inquiry into the Nature of Business Income under Present Price Levels (New York: American Institute of Accountants, 1949). Wm. A. Paton, "Measuring Profits under Inflation Conditions: A Serious Problem for Accountants," Journal of Accounting, LXXXIX, No. 1 (January, 1950), 16-27. Willard J. Graham, "The Effect of Changing Price Levels upon the Determination, Reporting and Interpretation of Income," Accounting Review, XXIV, No. 1 (January, 1949), 15-26. J.L. Dohr et al., "Depreciation and the Price Level," Accounting Review, XXIII, No. 2 (April, 1948), 115-136. Paul Grady, "A Proposal for the Adoption of Standards of Disclosure for Changing Price Levels," Journal of Accountancy, XCIV, No. 5 (November, 1952), 565-569. H.C. Greer and E.B. Wilcox, "The Case Against Price Level Adjustments in Income Determination," Journal of Accountancy, XC, No. 6 (December, 1950), 492-504. The Committee on Concepts and Standards Underlying Corporate Financial Statements, "Price Level Changes and Financial Statements," Accounting Review, XXVI, No. 4 (October, 1951), 469-474.

probe into the price level problem by relating the current controversy to the work of the security analyst.

When the price level was relatively stable, reported income was a meaningful mirror of over-all increments in physical resources (i.e., increases in cash, in inventory quantities, in units of plant and equipment). But the dramatic loss in the purchasing power of the dollar seems to have brought about a troublesome problem; reported income is no longer the indicative tool which it once was.[1] That is, the increments in assets reflected by reported income are often the same inventory quantities and the same or similar types of plant and equipment carried at higher dollar valuations. In other words, reported income is not the useful indicator of enhancement of distributable assets which it formerly was. "Accounting" income differs from "true," "real," or "economic" income.[2]

---

[1]The Committee on Concepts and Standards Underlying Corporate Financial Statements, op. cit., p. 468, point out: "Fluctuations in the United States Bureau of Labor Statistics Index of average for the year wholesale Prices:

1913 - 69.8	1939 - 77.1	1948 - 165.1
1920 - 154.4	1945 - 105.8	1949 - 155.0
1926 - 100.0	1946 - 121.1	1950 - 161.5
1932 - 64.8	1947 - 152.1	1951 - 182.8 (May)

[2]The tendency to use "true," "real" and "economic" income by writers favoring adjustments of the conventional accounting procedures of income determination is pointed out by E.B. Wilcox and H.C. Greer, op. cit., pp. 492-493: "Some writers have used the term 'real income' as distinguished from 'accountants' income.' It seems to follow that any other income is unreal, and should be discredited. This is bad semantics. We believe it is too clearly understood to need labored argument, that income is an artificial concept, not to be derived from a study of nature, and that the words 'real' or 'realistic' are no more than inappropriate emotionally charged words, the purpose of which can only be to call forth the conditioned response desired by their users. To say that income of any type or from any source is unreal, and should therefore be excluded from a concept of income, is to beg the question of what that concept of income should be."

The price level dispute becomes the most vivid in the area of fixed asset accounting. It is self-evident that in capital goods industries depreciation is almost always a significant amount. But even where depreciation is a small fraction of total expenses, it may be an important figure in comparison to net income. The argument for departing from the historical cost basis of recording fixed asset depreciation generally follows this line of reasoning:

> If we are charging into our costs depreciation on a plant built ten or fifteen years ago on the basis of its cost at that time, we are understating our costs and overstating our income on a current basis to the extent of the difference in the depreciation on present value of the machinery and equipment and depreciation on its cost at the time of acquisition.[1]

Willard Graham comments on the case for depreciation adjustments as follows:

> Depreciation on the basis of original costs charged to operations over the useful life of the assets--recovers--the <u>dollar</u> capital initially invested. Depreciation on the basis of current costs really charges against operations this same initial cost, measured, however, in terms of current dollars, thereby recovering the equivalent of the <u>physical</u> capital invested. Which of these is the more realistic interpretation of the concept of the amortization of actual cost? Certainly, the latter provides the better measure of the actual economic sacrifice incurred. It reflects a net income figure after provision for recovery of physical capital consumed. It avoids confusion of profits with a mere restatement of values in terms of the different monetary units. Any other concept of actual cost ceases to have significance when there is wide fluctuation in the value of the monetary unit in which the cost is measured and reported.[2]

The two leading approaches in departures from a historical cost basis of determining income are (a) that replacement costs should be charged against revenue or (b) that all historical costs which are to be matched against revenue should be adjusted

---

[1]Maurice E. Peloubet, in Dohr <u>et al</u>., <u>op. cit</u>., p. 124.

[2]Willard Graham, <u>op. cit</u>., p. 21.

on some common dollar basis so that all revenue and expenses may be expressed in dollars of the same (usually current) purchasing power. The proponents of the latter approach are not in agreement as to whether general price indexes or specific price indexes should be used in adjustments of historical dollar costs.

At this time none of the professional accounting organizations have officially advocated departures from the historical cost basis. They feel that any adjusted dollar statements should be supplementary to the conventional financial statements.[1]

Analysts' Concept of Income

When one considers the abundance of literature which has been produced in recent years concerning the impact of the changing price levels, it is startling to discover the universal antipathy on the part of the financial analysts toward the possible importance of measuring price level effects in financial reporting. Not <u>one</u> analyst who was interviewed attempts to adjust statements for price level changes. On the contrary, analysts seem to think in terms of dollars. The probable influence of the changing purchasing power of a 1938 dollar and a 1954 dollar is not considered to be relevant in analyzing specific financial data. The general attitude was succintly summarized by one prominent analyst who stated, "Price level? Oh, I suppose we plus or minus mentally for it."

---

[1]The Committee on Concepts and Standards Underlying Corporate Financial Statements, <u>op. cit.</u>, pp. 472-473. Committee on Accounting Procedure, American Institute of Accountants, <u>Accounting Research Bulletin No. 43: Restatement and Revision of Accounting Research Bulletins</u> (New York: American Institute of Accountants, 1953), pp. 67-71.

Depreciation Data

What the analysts do with depreciation data is significant and deserves appraisal because it indicates why price level adjustments are considered to be irrelevant.

As a passing comment in this discussion, it is noteworthy to point out the sloppy terminology used by analysts in referring to depreciation and amortization charges. Sentences such as the following are found frequently in analysts' reports: "Except for 1958, amortization and depreciation alone should generate substantially more than enough cash to meet all maturities of the present funded debt."[1]

The treatment of depreciation charges *as if* such allocations of original cost *generate* cash probably can be accepted *if* it always is kept in mind that such thinking is merely a short-cut calculation which is ultimately related to total funds received from the sale of goods to customers. However, sentences such as the one quoted above, calculations such as the ones below, and verbal comments by analysts lead this writer to wonder if there is a danger that analysts tend to believe that depreciation charges themselves generate cash. Such indications point toward the obligation of education in accounting and finance to clarify seemingly hazy thinking about the relationship between depreciation accounting and funds provided by *customers*. Terminology

---

[1]Jeremy C. Jenks, "Projecting Corporate Earnings," *The Analysts Journal*, IX, No. 1 (February, 1953), 100-101, offers the following observations: "One of the governing factors in a company's plant expansion program is the *availability of funds*. The amount of *cash that can be generated from* depreciation, depletion, and emergency amortization is fairly easily predictable. For example, Dow has about $175 million, net, of certificates which permit amortization at 20 per cent per year. Some of these plants will not be built, and so a figure of about $157 million may be used." (My italics.)

like "funds provided by depreciation" is erroneous and misleading description which should be abandoned completely.

Disregarding the difficulties of terminology, analysts' approaches with respect to depreciation reveal a definite pattern of thinking which discloses the reasons for their aversion toward price level adjustments.[1] Notice in the following excerpt from an analyst's probing of the Aluminum Company of America (Alcoa) the tendency (a) to think of depreciation as a cash flow[2] and (b) to relate depreciation and amortization to the debts which arose from capital expenditures and/or to new expenditures on plant. A similar analytical approach is illustrated in the five excerpts which follow this Alcoa analysis. All of these excerpts have been chosen because they exemplify the typical analytical techniques with regard to depreciation charges. The Alcoa example follows:

---

[1] B. Graham and D. Dodd, Security Analysis (3rd ed.; New York: McGraw-Hill, Inc., 1951), p. 130, refer to the problem of charging depreciation at other than original cost as follows: "From the standpoint of security analysis there may not be much difference involved in accepting either the original cost or a higher replacement cost as the basis value against which depreciation should be allowed. The higher-replacement-cost basis would result in decreasing the computed earnings in a given year, because of larger depreciation; but it would result, also, in increasing the assumed economic value of the assets--i.e., the book value of the stock. If both factors are given proper weight in arriving at a fair appraisal of a stock issue, the changes involved are likely to offset each other to a great extent."

[2] Jeremy C. Jenks, op. cit., p. 101, refers to depreciation in the following terms: "By 1954 to 1955 Monsanto and most other leading chemical companies may be generating more cash from depreciation, depletion, amortization, and retained earnings than will be needed for new plants, and accordingly, funds will then be available to reduce debt or for other purposes." (My italics.)

Millions	Debit Maturities		Estimated Amortization and Depreciation			
	Minimum	Optional	Amorti-zation	Depreci-ation	Total	Coverage of Min. Maturity
1953	$22.5		$33.2	$25.0	$58.2	2.6x
1954	24.0		45.6	27.0	72.6	3.0
1955-1958	(all details as above through 1959 as follows)					
1959	16.6	20.7	4.9	32.1	37.0	2.2

Amortization and depreciation alone should generate sufficient cash to meet all obligations of the present debt through 1959.

Notice the linking of depreciation with capital expenditures in the following excerpt from an analysis of the Chrysler Corporation:

> We understand that the bulk of the $250 million loan will be taken down this year. Chrysler's large expansion and modernization program may well require $100 million for plant and facilities in both 1954 and 1955. Depreciation provision for 1954 is estimated at about $55 million including roughly $15 million accelerated depreciation unallowable for FIT purposes. If the Revenue Act is changed in line with present suggestions, Chrysler may take the maximum allowable--probably equal to roughly its present provision. In any case, Chrysler's plant and equipment expenditures will probably exceed depreciation by a total of about $100 million over the next two years.

A further illustration of the analyst's approach to depreciation is found in the following excerpt from an analysis of E.I. Du Pont De Nemours and Company:

> Its cash flow from depreciation and amortization is now running at about $120 million annually. . . .
>
> Du Pont continues its capital expansion program which is very large in terms of dollars and even quite large in terms of du Pont itself (10-12 per cent of gross plant). Specifically, capital expenditures in 1953 were approximately $130 million. We estimate that expenditures for 1954 may be $135-$145 million. . . . Most of the required funds are coming from depreciation, including accelerated depreciation not allowable for income tax purposes. . . . We estimate that du Pont's total depreciation provision in 1954 will be $120-125 Million.

The following again illustrates the tendency to relate depreciation charges with debt retirement. This excerpt is taken from a comparative analysis of the aluminum industry:

> Although depreciation and amortization charges will be heavy during the next five years the fact that they will generate large cash earnings will facilitate orderly and rapid retirement of debt incurred to finance the expansion program. Alcoa, for instance, estimates that the company will accumulate enough cash through 1958 to permit the retirement of almost $300 million of senior obligations.

The following passage from the analysis of the Hercules Powder Company again exemplifies the analysts' inferences from depreciation data:

> For the five year ends 1952-48 cash and treasuries averaged 112 per cent of total current liabilities. At 12/31/53 this ratio was 110.2 per cent. Depreciation, amortization and retained earnings are indicated to be sufficiently sizable to handle the construction program this year without any material diminution of the very good cash assets to total current liabilities ratio. In the five years 1952-48 depreciation and retained earnings averaged $11.3 million, as compared with plant construction of $10.1 million per annum. Depreciation and retained earnings grew to $12.3 million in 1953, and are likely to be larger in 1954.

The application of "depreciation funds" to plant outlays is further illustrated in the following passage from the analysis of the Hooker Electrochemical Company:

> Depreciation, amortization and retained earnings are now indicated to be sufficiently sizable to handle presently authorized construction this year and next with only a moderate diminution of the excellent cash assets to total current liabilities ratio. In the five years 1953-49 depreciation and retained earnings averaged $3.3 million, rising to $3.9 million in 1953, as compared with average annual plant building of $7.6 million. This year depreciation, amortization and retained earnings are rising to an estimated $5.6 million, about in line with reported building authorizations.

Analysts' Reasoning

The above analysts' techniques with respect to depreciation, plus their unanimous aversion to index-number or replacement cost adjustments to historical cost methods of determining income, lead to speculation concerning the security analyst's concept of income.

If one attempts to apply the problems of changing price levels to the work of the analysts, he will find that the problems do not exist, at least directly, in their minds or in the way that they deal with financial data. The analyst evidently divides the revenue inflow from customers as if depreciation were that portion of revenue set aside for the purpose of capital expenditures.

A chart of the analyst's approach to the income statement could be drawn as follows:

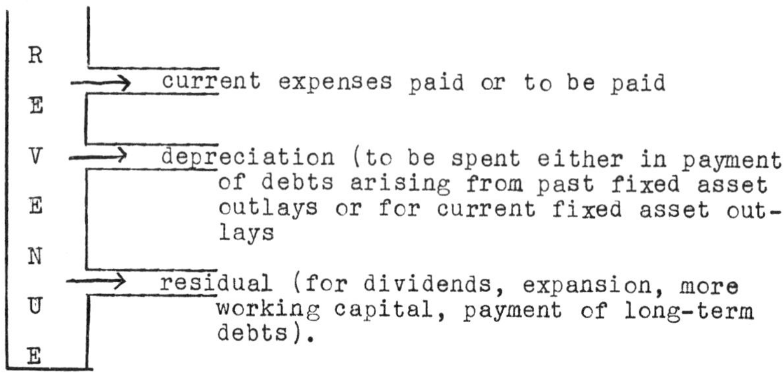

Thus the analyst's attitude toward income determination leans toward the following reasoning. Income is the difference between revenue from customers and the current costs of obtaining the revenue (materials, wages, utilities, advertising). Then the depreciation allocation is separated from this difference and should be devoted to capital expenditures or to the payment of debts arising from prior capital expenditures.[1] (Depreciation is

---

[1] John Ferguson, Jr., "Corporate Income Accounts," <u>The Analysts Journal</u>, IV, No. 1 (February, 1948), p. 11, states:

"something special" which is related to fixed asset outlays.)[1] The residual is available for dividends, further capital expenditures, payment of long-term debt, or expansion of working capital. Earnings as reported under conventional accounting, therefore, do not connote distributable earnings and are not thought of as such.

Really, if one considers the analyst's concept of income, the analyst is almost constantly thinking in terms of current dollars. Another look at the chart above will help to point out this fact. Revenue is in terms of current dollars, as are current expenses (with some exceptions in the case of widly fluctuating raw material prices coupled with fifo inventory methods). After the current expenses are funneled off, the difference is "what's left" of revenue (current dollars). A portion of this difference is considered to be "recovery" of past fixed asset outlays and is (or should be) devoted to paying off the long-term debt which arose from prior expenditures or else applied to maintaining or enhancing physical capacity. The final difference (residual) might be used in a variety of ways as indicated on the chart.

"Although a depreciation charge is not a cash outlay but merely a bookkeeping entry, it is a means by which a portion of current cash earnings may be conserved to replace that portion of a capital asset worn out during the period."

[1]Graham and Dodd, op. cit., p. 147, lend support to this kind of thinking with their concept of expended depreciation: "It may be proper to reduce depreciation to a figure approximating the average annual expenditure on plant additions and replacements over, say, ten to fifteen years in the past ('expended depreciation') . . . . The difference would then represent sums in addition to the surplus earnings which had flowed into working capital and thus presumably had been 'realized' for the benefit of stockholders. . . . It (expended depreciation) is found by subtracting the decrease in net plant account from the total depreciation charges for the period. . . . More simply, the 'unexpended depreciation' for a period is equal to the decrease in the net plant account during that period. (Substantial sales of property or write-downs charged to surplus would ordinarily be added back to plant in making this calculation.)"

This approach of the analyst, then, does emphasize current dollars and problems of the price level do not appear ominous to him. Consequently, he would be dismayed by attempts to recast the dollar into some other "adjusted" counter which might be meaningless or confusing in its application. Thus, as long as the analyst--and nearly everyone else--still thinks in terms of dollars (i.e., today's dollar--a dollar is a dollar is a dollar) the attempt to adjust the dollar via index numbers or some pseudo-replacement values merely offers a fuzzy concept in place of a workable, useful, and significant concept. Of course, if the purchasing power of the dollar eventually evaporates to the stage where people (and analysts) think of the dollar only in terms of the things it can buy, then the dollar concept will no longer be workable, useful, or significant.

Surely however, the above paragraphs do not intend to imply that the analyst does not keep in mind the value of the dollar in terms of the economic backdrop. The intelligent investor realizes that reported earnings are not distributable earnings. He is aware that simple replacement of productive facilities requires more dollars than are being "generated" by depreciation charges. So his analysis revolves about the impact of capital expenditure requirements upon future earnings and dividend-paying potentialities. After all, from the investor's vantage point, distributable earnings are earnings to be paid out in the form of dividends.[1] And in the valuation of securities probably one of

---

[1]Greer and Wilcox, op. cit., p. 503, have the following comments upon the purchasing-power-unit: "It follows even more forcefully that the purchasing-power-unit proposal offers little if any significance as to the financial ability of a company to

the factors explaining the historically weak price-earnings ratios (of 1947-1950) is that needs for capital outlays reduce dividend pay-out possibilities. This, then, is the "plus" or "minus" that the analyst applies in his allowance for price level changes.

Furthermore, when an analyst examines depreciation charges, he tends to appraise the amount of depreciation in terms of its "adequacy." In other words, depreciation sometimes is "inadequate" if the price level has changed substantially so that the depreciation amounts being charged are now insufficient to meet capital replacement demands. Certainly this is an example of how the analyst is cognizant of the changing price level. It also indicates the pattern of the analyst's thoughts concerning depreciation as that part of the current inflow of funds from customers that is or should be earmarked for capital expenditures.

Conclusion

It seems to this writer that accountants are increasingly recognizing that useful standards of a meaningful kind are positively necessary if accountancy is to perform successfully its important task in our economic system. In recent years the American Institute of Accountants, the American Accounting Association, and the Securities and Exchange Commission have progressed with giant steps toward the development of accounting standards. The past twenty years have been marked by substantial improvement in financial reporting, by improvement in auditing standards, and by improvement in the "independent" position of public accounting firms. But, as in every phase of business activity, there is an ever-widening and everlasting need for continued improvement. Accountants need to remember that analysts (and other readers) must examine hundreds or thousands of financial statements yearly. Thus accountants have a standing obligation to improve their products.

Accounting standards can provide a frame of reference for accounting practice. In turn, this frame of reference should be related to other bodies of knowledge and practice such as law, economics, and finance so that the network of such knowledge is strengthened by compelling consistency and universal applicability. Obviously, the latter relationships are the ideal. But it is toward the ideal that accounting practice should be directed. Detours or steps backward that add to confusion, to misinterpretations, to erroneous thinking, and to inconsistencies are routes which should be avoided.

Furthermore, it is apparent that the way in which accounting will develop will be evolutionary rather than revolutionary. The foremost reason for this condition is that there is no single authoritative accounting or government body which has (or probably will have) the inclination, the desire, or the power to "jar loose" the existing conventions, practices, and procedures from their foundations, however worthy of criticism the latter may be.

What is the ideal within the realm of accountancy? If it could be expressed in one clause, it is that financial statements must be structured for maximum usefulness. Moreover, usefulness requires unambiguous explanations and terminology, and information which is not misleading.

Judgment as to usefulness is made fundamentally by the

user, not the producer.[1] The analyst is the primary user of published financial statements. He represents, dollarwise, probably a very large percentage of existing investment capital. His negative reactions to price level adjustments, and the underlying reasons therefor, deserve much more recognition and scrutiny than they have received thus far.

---

[1]Study Group on Business Income, Changing Concepts of Business Income, op. cit., pp. 105, 108, et passim, apparently reached conclusions as to what is best for the investor without consulting the investor. William Werntz, as chief accountant of the Securities and Exchange Commission, dissented from the Study Group's conclusions as follows (p. 132) "Paragraph 25 is particularly susceptible to the implication that the cost statements now in general use are not desirable for the prospective investor. I believe, on the contrary, that they are useful, and that they should be the basic financial data furnished. . . . Whether such data (expressed in units of constant purchasing power) would be more or less useful to the prospective investor is a question not free from doubt."

CHAPTER IX

SUMMARY AND CONCLUSIONS

In attempting to use proper perspective in concluding this study the paraphrasing of the comments by Sidney Jacobsen, a trading specialist on the floor of the New York Stock Exchange seems significant:

> Security analysts perform necessary and important work. But their ideas of proper valuations of stocks are only their opinions. The general market consensus is often diametrically opposed to what analysts think should happen. For example, take the case of the Chance Vought Aircraft "spin-off" from United Aircraft earlier this year. My analyst friends, whose opinions I value highly, told me to expect a market price of $22 or $23 on that stock. Well, it almost immediately shot past $30 and right now it's at $33. I took a beating on that one, and it just goes to show you that the over-all market performance of an issue can often defy any rational analysis. It's what the thinking is here--reflecting the over-all market--that counts. If the public likes the glamour of a specific security, then any fancy analyses fall by the wayside.[1]

As is indicated above, it is a moot question whether or not the analyst will make better decisions concerning securities if he should receive corporate information in bigger and better quantities and qualities. The factors which are fused into a single investment decision are many and varied. Even the person or the committee making the decision often cannot present a systematic explanation of why decisions are made one way or the other. Words and phrases such as "progressive management," the

---

[1]Personal interview with Sidney Jacobsen, Trading Specialist, New York Stock Exchange, August 30, 1954.

"best industries," and "blue chips," are bandied about by professional investors without any common agreement as to the shades of meaning of such terms. Although investment analysis is a highly inexact activity, it does not follow that it is a useless endeavor. Most people probably would agree that without the legion of security analysts the capital markets would be much less orderly and much less stable than they now are.

Inasmuch as security analysts depend upon the quantitative information issued by accountants as part of the raw material which is related to the final investment decisions, accountants should recognize that financial reporting must be related to this purpose. The salient purpose of published accounting data is to serve investors better. In turn, how accounting can best accommodate investors depends upon their uses of financial information. This study has attempted to point out the more significant areas where investors feel that a better job might be accomplished.

The following points are the ones which appear to contain the most important implications for accountants of the uses of financial statements by security analysts:

1. Changing Price Level

Analysts are adamantly against any proposed "tampering" with conventional financial statements. They feel that the annual report should embrace the story of what has happened, and that financial statements themselves should tell a complete and detailed story of the financial impact of company activities expressed on a historical cost basis. They feel that any comments as to changes in purchasing power of today's dollar versus yesterday's dollar should not be embodied in the formal statements.

Obviously, analysts are also interested in what management's specific plans, hopes, and misgivings are for the future. But the latter information should not appear in the financial statements themselves.

It would seem that the accountants who are concerned about the impact of the dancing dollar upon the validity of conventional financial statements should consider the analyst's position on the over-all problem much more carefully than heretofore.

2. Fund Flows

It has been shown that analysts think of the operating statement in terms of fund flows of current dollars. It has also been pointed out that the analysis of balance sheets is chiefly concerned with the interrelationships of fund flows with respect to working capital needs, plant and equipment expenditures, capitalization structure, and dividend policies.

Analysts either draft a funds statement or analyze comparative balance sheets in such a way that their written words amount to a funds flow analysis. Analysts are particularly interested in capital expenditures. They always try to relate outlays for plant and equipment to future sales or profits or both.

Since the analyst finds a funds flow approach useful in examining both operating statements and balance sheets, it is evident that the accountant should supply a detailed funds statement in annual reports. The funds statement that now appears in only a few annual reports should be universally adopted as a part of the following trio of "must" presentations: (a) report of operations and reconciliation of retained earnings, (b) statement of funds, and (c) balance sheet. Also desirable would be a comparative statement of capital expenditures for the past five-to-seven years.

From the analyst's standpoint a statement of funds outranks the balance sheet in importance. The implication for accountants here is that much investigation into the area of the form and content of the funds statement is necessary. There has been a good deal of probing into the question in the past decade, and it is apparent that accounting education and research should devote more emphasis to the preparation and presentation of funds statements. Standards or working rules need to be formulated so that fund statements might be prepared upon some sound and uniform basis (much like present balance sheets and operating statements).

3. Comparison and Disclosure

The analyst's task is one of comparison. As investors or advisors to investors, analysts are entitled to adequate disclosure of corporate information in order that they might be better able to make intelligent decisions. They need details, especially with respect to operating statement items and capital expenditures, in order to facilitate comparisons.

Time-worn reasons for withholding financial information generally are no longer compelling. Because most of the data can be obtained anyway, more comprehensive disclosure is warranted in annual reporting. In this way all investors will rank abreast as far as availability of significant financial information is concerned.

Public accountants and controllers have an obligation to

do all that is within reason to persuade management to report more fully about the operations of the firm.

4. "Normalized" or "Sharp" Net Income

Analysts are firm in their demands for an income figure which "best reflects operations for the year." This writer feels that behind this request is some lack of comprehension of the utter impossibility of fulfilling such a demand satisfactorily. Net income is an opinion, not a fact. And opinions vary in almost direct proportion to the number of practising accountants. Therefore, as was outlined in Chapter VI, this writer does not see the feasibility of attempting to "sharpen" the net income residual as if it were the golden key which might unlock the analyst from his chamber of horrible operating data.

There is no panacea with respect to the analysis of financial statements. Attempts on the part of accountants to "normalize" net income can result only in perpetuating misconceptions about the apparent validity of such a figure and in adding to the Himalayan pile of confusion that accountants supposedly are trying to clarify.

The statement of operations should convey a reasonably detailed, complete, clear story of the financial impact of transactions upon the firm. The future lies ahead, and elements of possible forthcoming events do not belong in the body of the statement. The accountant's products should supply the analyst with a well-told story of the past accompanied by ample information (not in the body of the statement) concerning management's misgivings or hopes for the future. But the accountant is not and should not become a financial analyst. It is the analyst's task to determine "normal" or prospective earnings. Certainly the analyst should not be handicapped in his efforts by misleading or sketchy statements. That is why further disclosure and amplified descriptions are the most pressing problems of financial reporting today. Therefore, this writer believes that the suggested format (Chapter VI) for a "Statement of Operations and Reconciliation of Retained Earnings" is superior to any efforts toward drafting a statement leading to a figure labeled "net income," with its fictitious stamp of indelible finality.

5. Inventories

The implications for accountants with respect to the reporting of inventories are briefly outlined as follows:

(a) Revealing of the mere basis of valuation is not adequate disclosure. There should be careful and exacting description of the details of the valuation methods employed.

(b) Inventories should be broken down by major classes, by dollar amounts, and by methods of valuation.

(c) Where feasible, physical quantities should be disclosed. In this way price and quantity analysis may be facilitated.

(d) Where lifo, base stock, and similar methods of valuation are used, an estimate of current replacement cost should be disclosed.

(e) Where inventory reserves are used, full disclosure of the following points is essential: their origin, their function, their classification, and their yearly changes and adjustments.

6. Fixed Assets

The salient information which analysts desire with respect to fixed assets may be briefly summarized as follows:

(a) Past and planned capital expenditures together with descriptions of the types of equipment, products, and processes involved.

(b) Probable impact of capital expenditures on financial position, earnings and dividends.

(c) Thorough breakdown of fixed assets by classifications together with a short description of the depreciation accounting policies being applied.

(d) Thorough disclosure with respect to accounting for emergency facilities.

(e) More uniformity in depreciation policies within industries.

(f) Thorough disclosure of company obligations under long-term requirements.

Public accounting firms might review their own rather lax standards in approving statements which are sadly inadequate with respect to either points (d) or (f) above.

Conclusion

This study has sketched the analyst's approach to financial statements. Using his approach as a frame of reference, an appraisal of accounting trends and practices has been made. The appraisal has focused upon areas where improvements might be continued (i.e., more disclosure, more standardization, wider use of funds statements) and upon areas where accountancy might reappraise its current tendencies (i.e., toward "sharpening" net income, toward price level adjustments).

As a final note, it is emphasized that in general analysts are reasonably satisfied with the present form and content of corporate information. Analysts certainly are not raising loud protests about widespread deficiencies on the part of American companies. However as mentioned previously, in accountancy, as in every phase of business activity, there is an ever-widening and everlasting need for continued improvement. Accountants should remember that analysts must examine hundreds or thousands of financial statements yearly. Thus accountants have a standing obligation to improve their products.

Ideally financial statements must be constructed for maximum usefulness. Moreover, usefulness requires unambiguous explanations and terminology, and information which is not misleading.

Judgment as to usefulness is made ultimately by the user, not the producer. The analyst is the primary user of published financial statements. He represents, dollarwise, probably a very large percentage of existing investment capital. Analysts' opinions and procedures offer a source of valuable information that as yet has been tapped only lightly. Research in accountancy with respect to the serving of investors should give greater recognition to the analyst and should apply searching investigation to his position.

BIBLIOGRAPHY

Security Analysis and Accounting

Books

Alexander, S.S. Five Monographs on Business Income. New York: American Institute of Accountants, 1950.

Badger, Ralph, and Guthman, Harry. Investment Principles and Practices. 4th ed. New York: Prentice-Hall, Inc., 1951.

Butters, J.K. Effects of Taxation: Inventory Accounting and Policies. Boston: Harvard University Press, 1949.

Committee on Accounting Procedure, American Institute of Accountants. Accounting Research Bulletin No. 43: Restatement and Revision of Accounting Research Bulletins. New York: American Institute of Accountants, 1953.

Committee on Terminology, American Institute of Accountants. Accounting Terminology Bulletin No. 1. New York: American Institute of Accountants, 1953.

Committee on Corporate Information. Reports of National Committees for 1953. New York: New York Society of Security Analysts, Inc., 1954.

Cotter, Arundel. Fool's Profits. New York: Barron's Publishing Co., 1940.

Dean, A.H. Inquiry into the Nature of Business Income Under Present Price Levels. New York: American Institute of Accountants, 1949.

Dean, Joel. Managerial Economics. New York: Prentice-Hall, Inc., 1951.

Foulke, Roy. Study of the Theory of Corporate Net Profits. New York: Dun and Bradstreet, 1949.

________. Practical Financial Statement Analysis. New York: McGraw-Hill Book Co., Inc., 1950.

Gerstenberg, C.W. Financial Organization and Management of Business. New York: Prentice-Hall, Inc., 1939.

Graham, B., and Dodd, D. Security Analysis. 3rd ed. New York: McGraw-Hill Book Co., Inc., 1951.

Guthmann, Harry G. Analysis of Financial Statements. 4th ed. New York: Prentice-Hall, Inc., 1953.

May, George O. Business Income and Price Levels--An Accounting Study. New York: American Institute of Accountants, 1949.

Pickett, R., and Ketchum, M. Investment Principles and Policy. New York: Harper and Bros., 1954.

Prime, John H. Investment Analysis. New York: Prentice-Hall, Inc., 1952.

Study Group on Business Income. Changing Concepts of Business Income. New York: Macmillan Co., 1952.

Sweeney, H.W. Stabilized Accounting. New York: Harper and Bros., 1936.

Vatter, William J. Fund Theory of Accounting and Its Implications for Financial Reports. Chicago: University of Chicago Press, 1947.

________. Management Planning for Corporate Taxes. New York: Controllership Foundation, Inc., 1951.

Articles

Bailey, George. "Increasing Significance of the Income Statement," Journal of Accountancy, LXXXV (January, 1948), 10-12.

________. "Problems in Reporting Corporation Income," Harvard Business Review, XXVI (September, 1948), 682-686.

Blough, Carman G. "Accounting Reports and Their Meaning to the Public," Journal of Accountancy, LXVIII (September, 1939), 160-168.

________. "Lifo Inventory Accounting in a Period of Declining Prices," Analysts Journal, V (May, 1949), 12-14.

Bosic, Alex. "Patterns of Investment Research," Analysts Journal, V (May, 1949), 34-35.

Committee on Corporate Information. "Adequacy of the Annual Reports of the Chemical Industry," Analysts Journal, VI (May, 1950), 68.

________. "Fourth Annual Report," Analysts Journal, VIII (August, 1952), 70-71.

________. "Initial Report," Analysts Journal, X (February, 1954), 51.

________. "Second Annual Report," Analysts Journal, VI (May, 1950), 139-140.

________. "Third Annual Report," Analysts Journal, VII (May, 1951), 146-147.

Dohr, James. "Depreciation and the Price Level," Accounting Review, XC (July, 1950), 54-64.

________. "Materiality--What Does It Mean In Accounting?" Journal of Accountancy, XXIII (April, 1948), 115-136.

Frank, Jerome N. "Accounting for Investors," Journal of Accountancy, LXVIII (November, 1939), 300-307.

Galanis, J.M. "Shortcomings of Financial Statements from the Security Analyst's Viewpoint," Analysts Journal, III (November, 1947), 37-41.

Graham, Benjamin. "Financial Statements from the Viewpoint of the Financial Analyst," New York Certified Public Accountant XV (May, 1945), 235-239.

Graham, Willard J. "Effect of Changing Price Levels upon the Determination, Reporting, and Interpretation of Income," Accounting Review, XXIV (January, 1949), 15-26.

Greer, H.C., and Wilcox, H.B. "The Case Against Price Level Adjustments in Income Determination," Journal of Accountancy, XC (December, 1950), 495-504.

Jenks, Jeremy C. "Financial Community's Role in Stockholder Relations," Analysts Journal, IV (December, 1948), 36-38.

________. "Projecting Corporate Earnings," Analysts Journal, IX (February, 1953), 94-98.

Kaplan, Maurice, and Reaugh, Daniel. "Accounting Reports to Stockholders and the S.E.C." Accounting Review, XLV (September, 1939), 11-25.

Paton, William. "Measuring Profits Under Inflation Conditions," Journal of Accountancy, LXXXIX (January, 1950), 16-27.

________. "Shortcomings of Present-Day Financial Statements," Journal of Accountancy, LVII (February, 1934), 120-125.

Robbins, Carl B. "Business Secrets," Accounting Review, IV (June, 1929), 65-66.

Savage, Linwood. "Conclusions Regarding Annual Reports," Analysts Journal, X (February, 1954), 50-53.

Stiles, Albert I. "Corporate Management," Analysts Journal, III (September, 1947), 10-13.

Wilcox, E.B. "Rise and Fall of Lifo," Journal of Accountancy, LXXXV (February, 1948), 98-105.

THE DEVELOPMENT OF CONTEMPORARY ACCOUNTING THOUGHT

An Arno Press Collection

Baldwin, H[arry] G[len]. **Accounting for Value As Well as Original Cost** *and* Castenholz, William B. **A Solution to the Appreciation Problem.** 2 Vols. in 1. 1927/1931

Baxter, William. **Collected Papers on Accounting.** 1978

Brief, Richard P., Ed. **Selections from Encyclopaedia of Accounting, 1903.** 1978

Broaker, Frank and Richard M. Chapman. **The American Accountants' Manual.** 1897

Canning, John B. **The Economics of Accountancy.** 1929

Chatfield, Michael, Ed. **The English View of Accountant's Duties and Responsibilities.** 1978

Cole, William Morse. **The Fundamentals of Accounting.** 1921

Congress of Accountants. **Official Record of the Proceedings of the Congress of Accountants.** 1904

Cronhelm, F[rederick] W[illiam]. **Double Entry by Single.** 1818

Davidson, Sidney. **The Plant Accounting Regulations of the Federal Power Commission.** 1952

De Paula, F[rederic] R[udolf] M[ackley]. **Developments in Accounting.** 1948

Epstein, Marc Jay. **The Effect of Scientific Management on the Development of the Standard Cost System** (Doctoral Dissertation, University of Oregon, 1973). 1978

Esquerré, Paul-Joseph. **The Applied Theory of Accounts.** 1914

Fitzgerald, A[dolf] A[lexander]. **Current Accounting Trends.** 1952

Garner, S. Paul and Marilynn Hughes, Eds. **Readings on Accounting Development.** 1978

Haskins, Charles Waldo. **Business Education and Accountancy.** 1904

Hein, Leonard William. **The British Companies Acts and the Practice of Accountancy 1844-1962** (Doctoral Dissertation, University of California, Los Angeles, 1962). 1978

Hendriksen, Eldon S. **Capital Expenditures in the Steel Industry, 1900 to 1953** (Doctoral Dissertation, University of California, Berkeley, 1956). 1978

Holmes, William, Linda H. Kistler and Louis S. Corsini. **Three Centuries of Accounting in Massachusetts.** 1978

Horngren, Charles T. **Implications for Accountants of the Uses of Financial Statements by Security Analysts** (Doctoral Dissertation, University of Chicago, 1955). 1978

Horrigan, James O., Ed. **Financial Ratio Analysis—An Historical Perspective.** 1978

Jones, [Edward Thomas]. **Jones's English System of Book-keeping.** 1796

Lamden, Charles William. **The Securities and Exchange Commission** (Doctoral Dissertation, University of California, Berkeley, 1949). 1978

Langer, Russell Davis. **Accounting As A Variable in Mergers** (Doctoral Dissertation, University of California, Berkeley, 1976). 1978

Lewis, J. Slater. **The Commercial Organisation of Factories.** 1896

Littleton, A[nanias] C[harles] and B[asil] S. Yamey, Eds. **Studies in the History of Accounting.** 1956

Mair, John. **Book-keeping Moderniz'd.** 1793

Mann, Helen Scott. **Charles Ezra Sprague.** 1931

Marsh, C[hristopher] C[olumbus]. **The Theory and Practice of Bank Book-keeping.** 1856

Mitchell, William. **A New and Complete System of Book-keeping by an Improved Method of Double Entry.** 1796

Montgomery, Robert H. **Fifty Years of Accountancy.** 1939

Moonitz, Maurice. **The Entity Theory of Consolidated Statements.** 1951

Moonitz, Maurice, Ed. **Three Contributions to the Development of Accounting Thought.** 1978

Murray, David. **Chapters in the History of Bookkeeping, Accountancy & Commercial Arithmetic.** 1930

Nicholson, J[erome] Lee. **Cost Accounting.** 1913

Paton, William Andrew and Russell Alger Stevenson. **Principles of Accounting.** 1918

Pixley, Francis W[illiam]. **The Profession of a Chartered Accountant and Other Lectures.** 1897

Preinreich, Gabriel A. D. **The Nature of Dividends.** 1935

Previts, Gary John, Ed. **Early 20th Century Developments in American Accounting Thought.** 1978

Ronen, Joshua and George H. Sorter. **Relevant Financial Statements.** 1978

Shenkir, William G., Ed. **Carman G. Blough: His Professional Career and Accounting Thought.** 1978

Simpson, Kemper. **Economics for the Accountant.** 1921

Sneed, Florence R. **Parallelism in Two Disciplines.** (M.A. Thesis, University of Texas, Arlington, 1974). 1978

Sorter, George H. **The Boundaries of the Accounting Universe** (Doctoral Dissertation, University of Chicago, 1963). 1978

Storey, Reed K[arl]. **Matching Revenues with Costs** (Doctoral Dissertation, University of California, Berkeley, 1958). 1978

Sweeney, Henry W[hitcomb]. **Stabilized Accounting.** 1936

Van de Linde, Gérard. **Reminiscences.** 1917

Vatter, William J[oseph]. **The Fund Theory of Accounting and Its Implications for Financial Reports.** 1947

Walker, R. G. **Consolidated Statements.** 1978

Webster, Norman E., Comp. **The American Association of Public Accountants.** 1954

Wells, M. C., Ed. **American Engineers' Contributions to Cost Accounting.** 1978

Worthington, Beresford. **Professional Accountants.** 1895

Yamey, Basil S. **Essays on the History of Accounting.** 1978

Yamey, Basil S., Ed. **The Historical Development of Accounting.** 1978

Yang, J[u] M[ei]. **Goodwill and Other Intangibles.** 1927

Zeff, Stephen Addam. **A Critical Examination of the Orientation Postulate in Accounting, with Particular Attention to its Historical Development** (Doctoral Dissertation, University of Michigan, 1961). 1978

Zeff, Stephen A., Ed. **Selected Dickinson Lectures in Accounting.** 1978